50 Tools
for
Building Brilliant Schools

A Workbook for School Leaders
to Transform Culture and Performance

by Dr. Andy Parker

Companion to *Building Brilliant Schools: What G.R.E.A.T. Leaders Do Differently* © 2021

GLOBAL WELLNESS MEDIA
STRATEGIC EDGE INNOVATIONS PUBLISHING
LOS ANGELES, TORONTO, MONTREAL

First Edition. Published by:
Global Wellness Media
Strategic Edge Innovations Publishing
340 S. Lemon Ave #2027
Walnut, California 91789-2706
(866) 467-9090
StrategicEdgeInnovations.com

Editor: Marjorie Frank
Book Designer: Mary Bullock
Cover Designer: Global Wellness Media

Title: 50 Tools for Building Brilliant Schools
Subtitle: A Workbook for School Leaders to Transform Culture and Performance
ISBN: 978-1-957343-99-0

Contents

About *50 Tools for Building Brilliant Schools*

Why?

This book, *50 Tools for Building Brilliant Schools,* is a companion to the handbook, *Building Brilliant Schools: What G.R.E.A.T. Leaders Do Differently*. That book is a guide that identifies critical underpinnings for a successful school and outlines a pathway for leaders to construct and maintain those foundations. Throughout my years of experience as a teacher, school leader, leadership coach, and mentor, I've spent a lot of time pondering the question of what makes a brilliant school. I've noticed recurring assumptions, priorities, and actions that served as a firm base for a flourishing, excellent educational setting. I've gathered these into what I call pillars—broad, deep, sound structures that, together, can transform struggling schools into thriving, engaging, student-centered, equitable places of learning. They can also turn fairly successful schools into brilliantly successful schools. These pillars are:

Gratitude—noticing, understanding, and actively appreciating people and situations

Relationships—the real, trusting, and reliable connections with others

Expectations—the assumptions, intentions, and possibilities we project to each other

Achievement—what we believe and how we act to help each other attain at best levels

Tenacity—how we keep trying, working, adapting, and hoping—without giving up

That first book, *Building Brilliant Schools*, defines and explains (with research-backed findings) each of the G.R.E.A.T. pillars. In addition, it gives details about the benefits, obstacles, interventions, attitudes, and behaviors that build and sustain each pillar. It is filled with mindsets, concrete steps, and actions to help leaders and other educators get results with each pillar.

But wait! I wanted to provide even more of the practical, how-to-get-it-done assistance than is contained in that book. I wanted leaders, teachers, and students to have hands-on instruction in **doing** the kinds of strategies that propel the building of a brilliant school.

What?

So here is the result! When the first book was finished, I jumped right into this workbook. It's a collection of practical tools to guide leaders and other educators step-by-step through some powerful practices that assemble, expand, and strengthen the pillars of **Gratitude**, positive **Relationships**, high and equal **Expectations**, increased **Achievement**, and academic **Tenacity**. By "workbook" I mean: You work right in this book. It's designed for you to reflect, create, make notes, write questions, and add ideas as you follow the steps to use each tool.

- The workbook has **five chapters**—each one focused on one of the G.R.E.A.T. pillars.

- Each chapter begins with a **brief overview of the pillar:** its definition, the key benefits of building that tool, and a condensed list of key research-based practices and attitudes shown to lead to all the possible benefits for students and school communities.

- The overview of each chapter is followed by **10 tools**—each one focused on a research-based practice or intervention proven to help schools make gains in building and sustaining that pillar. In the description of each tool, you will find

  ◦ Its purpose

  ◦ Indication of who will use the tool (the audience)

  ◦ Background information about the topic and purpose

  ◦ Supplies needed for the tool

  ◦ Resources for the leader, including reference to the pages in *Building Brilliant Schools: What G.R.E.A.T. Leaders Do Differently,* that expand information about the topic

  ◦ Clear steps for DOING the process or strategy

  ◦ One or more worksheets—reproducible graphic pages (a form, graphic organizer, checklist, table, reflection, working guide, etc.) for users to complete or follow as part of the steps for DOING the strategy

  ◦ A final evaluation tool—a place to reflect on your experiences of using the tools in each chapter

Who?

As you begin to read and work with the tools, you will note that they have a wide range of uses—and can involve many members of the school community. Some tools are aimed at specific audiences. Many have uses, with adaptation, for several audiences. The audiences are

- School leaders
- Teachers
- Other staff members
- Students
- Parents

Note: Many of the tools can be used by more than one of these groups.

Note: Several of the tools have components where individuals work alone at a strategy, but even then, most tools include some collaboration.

When? and Where?

Just as the audiences are broad, so are the places and times when the tools can be effectively used. Depending on the tool, it can be used when and where . . .

- Leaders are learning together
- Leaders are training teachers or other staff
- Educators are learning together in professional development sessions, team meetings, faculty meetings, or grade-level meetings
- Teachers or other staff members are learning cooperatively in any setting
- Teachers are working on these practices with students
- Students are working together to strengthen one of the pillars
- Parents are involved in learning with and supporting school staff or students

Note: Most of the tools can be used in more than one of these settings.

How?

There are various ways to use the workbook. In general, the workbook is designed for situations where leaders would be guiding teachers or other staff members through the steps. However, this is rather fluid—because, after first learning the tool, the participants may be reading and following the steps---or even guiding others through them. As a professional development guide, a group of leaders or school staff members might work through the workbook one chapter at a time—sequentially through the tools. Or, leaders or teachers may focus on one pillar that needs particular focus. Individuals or groups might tackle one tool, chosen to fit a specific school improvement goal or team or grade-level goal.

These "how-to-use-the-tools" guidelines, thus, are for whatever person is doing the leading—and for whatever approach is needed.

Before using a tool:

- Be aware that the word *students* not only refers to kids. Anyone involved with the use of a tool is a *student*—including the facilitator of the process.

- Read through every tool thoroughly and gather the supplies and resources before leading a group in its use.

- Read the chapters from *Building Brilliant Schools: What G.R.E.A.T. Leaders Do Differently* indicated in the tool's introduction so that you are familiar with the pillar, concepts, research, interventions, and applications.

- DO every activity ahead of time, if possible. But for sure, do it **along with** the participants in your group (even if you tried it out beforehand).

- Be the model for how your participants will use the tool with their students.

- Be ready to be vulnerable. When an activity is a bit threatening or uncomfortable—you go first with a genuine (never artificially-contrived or made up) personal example.

- Be ready to be open to feedback from your group. Be brave! Part of building a brilliant school is forging trusting relationships—especially those in which members can trust their leaders and give honest feedback.

- Plan for adapting the steps or the graphic worksheet to your group, as needed.

During the process:

- Take the time needed with each step. Allow time for participants to try, question, share, and digest the process. Make adaptations "on the fly" where they are needed.

- Include time for questions and discussion where indicated or needed.

- Always invite students (of any age) to write or suggest other ideas; they can use these (substitute them, add them) as they follow the strategy.

- Watch and listen! Jot down notes about responses, ideas, and insights that you have or gather from participants. These will help you broaden the experience or make adjustments for the next use of the tool. Write these on the workbook pages.

Wrapping up the process, and even after that:

- Ask for feedback from the participants. Find out what students learned, what was meaningful or helpful, what they will remember and continue to do.

- Ask, "What next?" "What else?" "Where can we go from here?" "How can we apply this?" "Where will we use this?" With most tools, it will be helpful to have a general or specific plan for next steps—for what you all will do with what you learned.

- Ask for and keep track of alternatives for using the tool again—how to change it, how to apply it to other situations, etc.

- Later (next week, etc.), revisit participants to check up on the longer-term effects or outcomes (Ask: "How are the tools working?" "Which ones have you used?" "What have you adapted and how?" "How are your students (or teachers) responding?")

- The tools in the workbook include graphic worksheets. Once leaders, teachers, or kids use these—they'll have ideas for adaptations or for creating their own. Kids will love this. Teachers will feel empowered. Be sure to use the worksheets they concoct!

- Keep folders of products. These would be completed worksheets or other "products" that result from using the tools. Find ways to make use of these products.

- Every chapter (pillar) ends with an evaluation tool. It guides users in a reflection on the tools from that pillar and how they worked. Revisit these evaluations often.

- Use tools across the pillars. Most tools have applications to concepts, actions, or needs in more than one pillar. Be on lookout for ways to apply the tool to other pillars.

Contact the Author

I'm eager to learn about what works for you as you use this book. Please feel free to send me messages, questions, or suggestions. Tell me about your experiences with the tools, and what new ideas or outcomes they have inspired.

Contact me at **drandy@drandyparker.com**

To learn more about my G.R.E.A.T. Leadership Philosophy (TM)—and to **receive a free chapter from the handbook,** *Building Brilliant Schools: What G.R.E.A.T. Leaders Do Differently*—go to **www.drandyparker.com/book**

Dr. Andy Parker

Chapter 1

Tools for Your **GRATITUDE** Toolbox

Gratitude is not only the greatest of virtues but the parent of all others.

– Marcus Tullius Cicero

This collection of tools focuses on the researched-based traits, skills, or practices that have been identified as key influences on the development of gratitude and on the numerous benefits that follow from regular gratitude practice.

⚙ Definitions

Gratitude:
> *a two-step cognitive process*
> (a) recognizing that one has obtained a positive outcome, and
> (b) recognizing that there is an external source for this positive outcome
> (Emmons & McCullough, 2003. p. 378)

Gratitude:
> *an act of giving back out of acknowledgment for what we received*
> (Howells, 2013, p. 1).

⚙ Key Benefits of Gratitude

People (of all ages) who recognize and express gratitude (in comparison to those who show less gratitude) exhibit higher levels of:

- Social integration and friendships
- Prosocial behavior (and decreases in antisocial behavior)
- Greater job satisfaction and job effectiveness
- Motivation to use abilities and strengths to help others
- Building strong and satisfying connections to others
- Self-regulation, self-respect, and self-satisfaction
- Sense of purpose
- Generosity
- Empathy and patience
- Hope and resilience
- Positive affect
- Interest in helping others
- Overall psychological well-being and general life satisfaction

Practicing gratitude also increases resilience and diminishes resentment and negativity. It leads to greater appreciation for one's co-workers and helps workers handle the stresses of their work. Profoundly, people who practice gratitude are far more likely to show caring, accepting, helpful attitudes and behaviors toward others.

For students in a school setting, it's found that those who can express gratitude have greater:

- Interest in school
- School connectedness and sense of well-being at school
- Academic success (including higher GPAs for adolescents)
- Strong social ties at school and more positive motivations toward others
- Absorption (full engagement in learning activities)
- Social-emotional learning skills and self-regulation in school activities
- Ability to set and pursue meaningful, intrinsic goals
- Kind and helpful behavior

Research has also found that gratitude in young people reduces levels of aggression and other antisocial behaviors. It diminishes cheating, combats materialism, buffers students from stress and depression, and supports resilience.

⚙ Interventions that Increase Gratitude

Parents, teachers, and other adults can help young people build gratitude. Adults can work to build gratitude in themselves and collaborate with colleagues in expression of gratitude. All of us have access to the amazing benefits listed above. And studies show that gratitude inventions have profound and long-lasting effects, including neural effects. The brain has sort of "a gratitude muscle" that can be exercised and strengthened.

Gratitude intervention involves:

- Intentional, ongoing experiences of gratitude awareness
- Multiple, targeted, repeated opportunities for children (or adults) to express gratitude
- Teaching students the language and actions of gratitude
- Doing—the conscious, purposeful act of noticing things and people for which one is grateful and acting on that knowledge

Be aware that the concept of a *practice* involves a conscious and purposeful act that we repeat.

Note: For a more complete discussion of gratitude definitions, benefits, and interventions, see Chapters 1 through 4 in *Building Brilliant Schools: What G.R.E.A.T. Leaders Do Differently*, by Dr. Andy Parker (2021).

Use the next page to keep notes from your reading of those chapters.

⚙ Gratitude Tools for Brilliant Schools

Each of the following tools included in this chapter teaches or strengthens one or more of the researched-based skills known to nurture gratitude.

1. Gratitude Infusion (Gratitude Modeling by Leader)

2. Yes-Brain Boosters (Priming the Brain for Gratitude)

3. Counting Blessings (Gratitude Awareness)

4. Gratitude Spies (Gratitude Awareness)

5. Gratitude Journals (Gratitude Awareness and Expression)

6. Putting It into Words (Gratitude Expression)

7. The Art of Gratitude (Gratitude Expression)

8. Gratitude Circles (Gratitude Expression; Class Unity)

9. Gratitude Risk-Benefit Practice (Gratitude Analysis)

10. Reflecting on the Tools (Self-evaluation of Use of Gratitude Tools)

Notes from Gratitude Chapters

Building Brilliant Schools: What G.R.E.A.T. Leaders Do Differently, Chapters 1–4

As you read about Gratitude, jot down key ideas or points that you want to remember from each chapter.

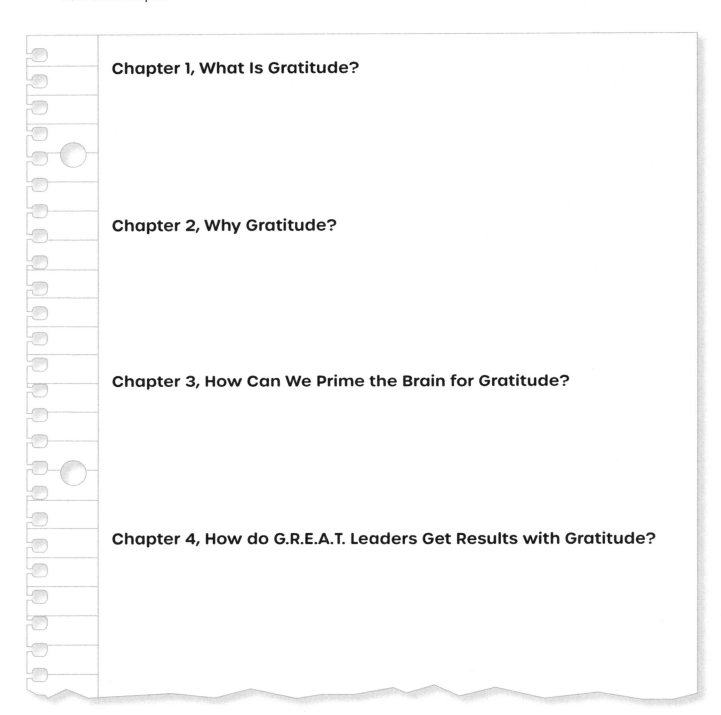

Chapter 1, What Is Gratitude?

Chapter 2, Why Gratitude?

Chapter 3, How Can We Prime the Brain for Gratitude?

Chapter 4, How do G.R.E.A.T. Leaders Get Results with Gratitude?

Tool 1   GRATITUDE INFUSION

 Purpose: Introduce the school community to gratitude and its expression

 User(s): School leaders

Leader Resources:

> *Building Brilliant Schools* by Dr. Andy Parker (2021), Chapters 1, 2, and 4
> Other background articles, research, or resources the leader has gathered

Supplies:

> Worksheet G.1, Leader's Gratitude Plan

Description:

Gratitude might not be the first component that comes to mind when you think about pillars upon which to build your school culture. That's likely because most educators weren't trained in teacher prep programs or in our own school experience to rely on gratitude. But with all the striking discoveries about what gratitude can do for students and a school culture, school leaders are in just the right position to ignite gratitude awareness and practice. This tool gives leaders some ideas about how to dive right in, as soon as the staff and students return to school, to introduce the ambiance and practice of gratitude to the school community. You don't need to have any formal plans made or any programs set up. Just let your convictions and passion start spreading gratitude. You'll notice—in a few short weeks—that everyone in the school (and the students' families, too) starts to catch on. They hear, and see in action, the workings of gratitude. But of course, you'll want this awareness to grow and permeate your school life until it becomes a solid, lasting cornerstone of the culture. So, this is just the beginning—and oh, what a beginning! It's amazing what a stage of positivity this sets.

Steps:

1. Use the template on **Worksheet G.1, Leader's Gratitude Plan**, to gather ideas about how you will model and infuse gratitude practices right away.

2. The categories on Worksheet G.1 correspond to ideas below described from Dr. Andy's experience (in his role as school leader). Scan through his shared experiences. Use them to ignite and gather your ideas and plans for what you'll do in these categories. For each category, ask yourself: *How will I do this? When? Where? Whose help can I enlist?*

Dr. Andy's Experiences:

1. **Gratitude for Students**—I modeled gratitude to my students during assemblies and my communications with them each day. I regularly let them know that I was grateful to be their leader.

2. **Gratitude for Staff Members**—I modeled gratitude for my teachers and other school staff members in afterschool meetings, in daily announcements, and in personal contacts. I regularly let them know that I was grateful to be their colleague and friend.

3. **Gratitude for Students' Parents**—I modeled gratitude to parents in every situation where I could see, visit with, or in any way communicate with students' families. I regularly mentioned my gratitude for parents when speaking to staff and students.

4. **Gratitude for the Community**—I made a quick list of persons and organizations beyond our school walls who contributed to the school in some way. Then I made phone calls or sent texts, emails, or notes to express gratitude.

5. **All-School Daily Gratitude Routines**—Before school started, I set up a Gratitude Jar in the main office. I invited staff and students to drop entries into the jar—naming a person (friend, classmate, teacher, custodian, etc.) for whom they were grateful and briefly explaining why. Each day, we pulled some entries from the jar and read them over the intercom during afternoon announcements. (See Gratitude Jars in Tool 6.)

6. **Yearly Gratitude Theme**—I started the practice of organizing the school year around a positive theme that incorporated gratitude (supported by graphics throughout the school). One theme was "One Degree More"—the idea of pushing everyone to give one degree more in all academic, personal, and social school experiences. We kicked off the theme with a video about water boiling at 212°F, showing how that one-degree difference from 211°F gets a different result. We built a tagline into morning and afternoon announcements that reminded everyone to give one degree more. We used this theme in all meetings and connections with colleagues, students, and parents. We asked everyone to notice and express gratitude for those who in some way helped them give *one degree* more!

7. **All-School Gratitude Definition**—A school-wide understanding of what gratitude is serves as a foundation for your efforts to spread gratitude. I wanted to give my own modeling a bit of time to "sink" in, but had already formed a plan and process to gather input from students, staff, parents, and leaders to create our definition of gratitude.

Name _____

Leader's Gratitude Plan

How will you spread gratitude from the moment school events (or before-school events) begin? Write your ideas and intentions for how (and when and where) you will do or show this. Include one or two clear plans for each category.

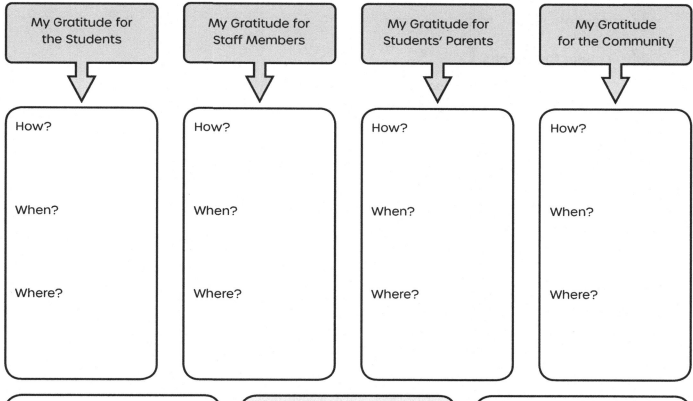

My Gratitude for the Students	My Gratitude for Staff Members	My Gratitude for Students' Parents	My Gratitude for the Community
How? When? Where?	How? When? Where?	How? When? Where?	How? When? Where?

All-School Daily Gratitude Routines	Gratitude Theme	All-School Gratitude Definition

Tool 2   YES-BRAIN BOOSTERS

 Purpose: Help staff members and students move from No-brain states to Yes-brain states

 User(s): Leaders, teachers, students

Leader Resources:

>*Building Brilliant Schools* by Dr. Andy Parker, (2021), Chapter 3
>
>Research of Dan Siegel and his co-author and co-researcher Tina Payne Bryson

Supplies:

>Worksheet G.2a, Trading No for Yes (for Leaders and Teachers)
>
>Worksheet G.2b, The Great Brain Switch (for Students)
>
>Notebooks or other paper for recording Yes and No impressions
>
>Pens or pencils
>
>Poster paper or whiteboard and markers

Description:

Remember that while gratitude involves feelings, it is also a cognitive process. It is something you examine and think about. To grow the skills of gratitude, we all need to hone the skills of self-awareness and examination of how we think (called *mindsight*). Part of mindsight is noticing when you are in a No-brain state or a Yes-brain state, as described in the work of Dr. Dan Siegel and Tina Payne Bryson (2018).

The Yes-brain state is open, receptive, resilient, and proactive. It's connected to sensations of calm, hopefulness, possibilities, motivation, and caring. The No-brain state is shut down and reactive. It's connected to sensations of tightness, resistance, powerlessness, and fear. One of the proven ways to open ourselves to noticing, expressing, and receiving gratitude is to develop skills that help bring balance to the brain—shifting away from the No-brain state. This is a process that takes practice and time. With this tool, leaders, teachers, and students can take some concrete steps toward that practice.

Steps for Leaders or Leaders and Staff Together:

1. Learn about Yes-brain and No-brain states.

   • Use the resources above to learn as much as you can about the Yes-brain concept and research.

   • Begin to pay attention to your own No-brain or Yes-brain thoughts and actions.

2. Leaders, introduce your staff to the concept of Yes-brain and No-brain states and thinking. Begin with this activity (supplying note pads, pens/pencils, and poster paper on a wall):

   • Gather the staff together. Eliminate all distractions that you can (phones, screens, etc).

   • Tell group members that you'll say a word to them, and ask them to pay close attention to how they respond to hearing it. Tell them to notice their physical responses (muscle tightness, pulse rate, etc.); to notice and name their feelings; and to notice what thoughts, words, phrases, or ideas come to their minds.

   • Ask them to close their eyes. Wait a few moments. Say "NO!" loudly and harshly. (OR, you could say NO to something specific you know they have been hoping for—such as "I need to inform you that there will be NO extra planning time for teachers this year!")

   • Tell them to open their eyes and jot down things they've noticed. If need be, give quiet prompts: *Notice your pulse rate . . . any tension . . . mood . . . words . . .thoughts.*

   • Share their impressions. A couple of volunteers can record these on the poster paper.

Take a break. Stretch.

   • Repeat the process. This time, say "YES!" with warmth and enthusiasm.

   • Record and share the responses. Compare them to the "NO" responses.

   • Share information that you've learned about Yes-brain states and No-brain states.

3. Ask staff members to start paying attention to their own brain states—to notice when their thinking or actions come out of a No-brain or Yes-brain state. Ask them to think about what kinds of things they tend to respond to with NO or their actions or responses that regularly come out of a No-brain state. They can then use **Worksheet G.2a, Trading No for Yes**, to note some of their No-Brain responses (internal thoughts and responses and outward responses).

4. Set an assignment or process for taking the next step of rethinking, reworking, and rewording to change NO responses into YES responses. Ask them to think of ways they can include "Yes" to some part or all of the situation. They can do this individually or in pairs.

5. Find a time for them to share and discuss their experiences with this process. Repeat this process over time until everyone gets better at it. Brainstorm to help each other with ideas for making the switch. Be sure to do this in groups of leaders, as well.

Steps for Teachers to Do with Students:

1. Find a way to introduce the idea of Yes-brain and No-brain states to students. The activity on the previous page works well with several age groups.

2. The first part of the process with students is helping them notice when they are in a No-brain state and trying to identify how they got there. Ask kids to think of times, places, situations, assignments, events, etc. in which they feel the physical and mental NO responses. Students can brainstorm and role-play ways to react to or ride out restrictive, frightened feelings.

3. Work up to helping students identify and discuss sensations they feel (or sense that others feel) in a particular, tense or important situation. They can write words, draw or describe images, or describe thoughts that accompany the situation. As they become more aware of their inner lives, kids will be more able to balance their responses and regulate their behavior.

4. Researchers have found that it is only with identifying, acknowledging, and accepting what they find in themselves that persons can handle, let go of, or transform their responses. So keep practicing this with students.

5. Researchers have also found that people can take specific measures to switch from a No-brain to a Yes-brain state. Children benefit immensely from learning and practicing techniques to balance themselves out when they fall into the grip of a No-brain state. The activity on **Worksheet G.2b, The Great Brain Switch**, is an example of this.

Other things that help kids balance out a No-brain state and switch to a Yes-brain state (or catching themselves headed in a No-brain direction and stopping the trajectory) are:

- Being in the presence of safety, empathy, and connection
- Naming the emotion and then seeing if they can balance it out by describing how it is affecting them
- Taking the perspective of someone else who's in the situation
- Moving—stretch, dance, do jumping jacks, or get other exercise
- Reaching out to care for someone else who's having a hard time
- Learning to notice signs that they are heading for a No-brain state

Use this activity many times.

Name _____

Trading No for Yes

List situations, processes, practices, or actions that have triggered or might trigger a No-brain response. Describe that response. Then describe a response that would flow, instead, from a Yes-brain state.

Topic, Idea, Process, Practice, Action	Your No-Brain Response	Your Yes-Brain Response

The Great Brain Switch

Name a situation that has put you in a No-brain state. Write it on this gloomy cloud.

Words or pictures that describe how this feels:

Make the Switch!

1. Breathe in slowly as you count to 4.

2. Hold for count of 1.

3. Breathe out slowly as you count to 4.

4. Hold for a count of 1.

5. Think of one of these:
   good experience you have recently had
   something you are good at doing
   something you are proud of

6. Describe that in the sunburst.

7. Now focus on that for 1 minute.
   Close your eyes. Breathe in and out slowly.
   Picture yourself doing what you wrote about.
   Enjoy feeling grateful for that RIGHT NOW.

8. Open your eyes and say YES!

Words or pictures that describe how this feels:

Tool 3   COUNTING BLESSINGS

⊛ **Purpose:** Increase gratitude awareness

 User(s): Leaders, teachers, students

 Leader Resource:

> *Building Brilliant Schools* by Dr. Andy Parker (2021), Chapters 1, 2, and 4

📝 **Supplies:**

> Worksheet G.3a, Count Your Blessings!
> Worksheet G.3b, The Grateful-Brain Map

Description:

"Count your blessings" is an adage that has been around for a long time—for good reason. Research shows how positive the impacts of counting your blessings can be. For In a randomized trial of a "counting blessings" intervention, researchers found that people who wrote about their blessings weekly for 10 weeks or daily for 14 days reported feeling more optimistic about each following week. Also, they were more likely to report helping someone. Neuroscience research has found that, with more gratitude practice, the brain strengthens pathways that can help a person automatically feel more positive and grateful in the future.

This tool gives leaders, teachers, and students a simple strategy to slow down and notice the fortunes in their lives.

Steps:

1. This can be done by anyone of any age: Think back over your week: What special benefits, favors, approvals, good wishes, caring acts, or favorable circumstances have come your way this week?

2. Use **Worksheet G.3a, Count Your Blessings,** to briefly describe three or four blessings. Identify the source of each blessing.

3. Do this once a week.

4. Teachers should regularly let students know that expressing gratitude releases brain chemicals that improve their mood and help them feel happier. Students will be interested to know that the more they practice it, the more gratitude they will be able to feel and express to others. This knowledge is a good bridge to the use of brain maps for counting blessings. (See next step.)

5. For another way to notice and record blessings, make a brain map. Follow the directions on **Worksheet G.3b, The Grateful-Brain Map**. Start with an outline of your head or a drawing of a brain and note blessings in several components of your life.

6. Alternative ways to count blessings. Here are a few examples from schools in the district where I was an administrator:

   • Some teachers asked students to write a blessing every day or every other day. They felt that this got their students in a regular habit of noticing blessings.

   • In many of our kindergarten, first-grade, and second-grade classrooms, teachers showed kids how to count their blessings across their fingers. This became a daily habit they incorporated into morning class meetings or into their end-of-the-day class circles.

   • When scooping macaroni and cheese or putting squares of pizza on lunch trays, one of our beloved cafeteria ladies said, daily, to kids in the line, "Let's count our blessings," She'd hold up a gloved hand and count: one, two, three, and state some of her blessings. Kids voiced theirs at the same time. This cafeteria-line ritual became something kids enjoyed and looked forward to each afternoon. It set a wonderful tone for the second half of the day!

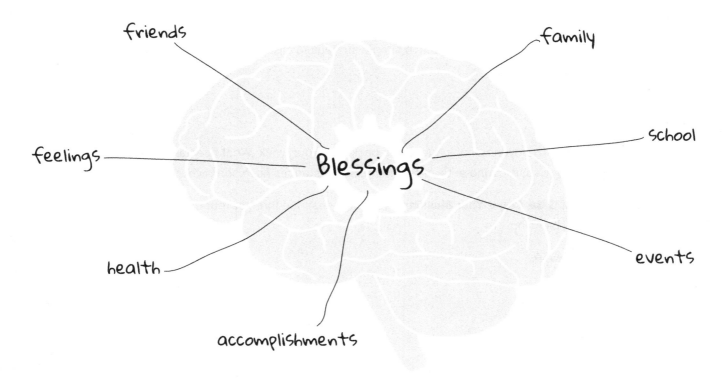

Count Your Blessings!

Think back over the past week and write down three or four things for which you are grateful or thankful.

What's the source? Think about where the blessing came from. If there is a person, (or persons), place, or other source you can identify, write it (or them) beneath the thought bubble.

_____　　_____

_____　　_____

Name _____

The Grateful-Brain Map

1. Write BLESSINGS in the center of the brain image.

2. Draw lines (spokes) out from the word. Label the end of each line with some component of life (such as family, friends, school, events, health, mental health, accomplishments, feelings).

3. On each line, write one or more things (related to that topic) that inspire gratitude for you.

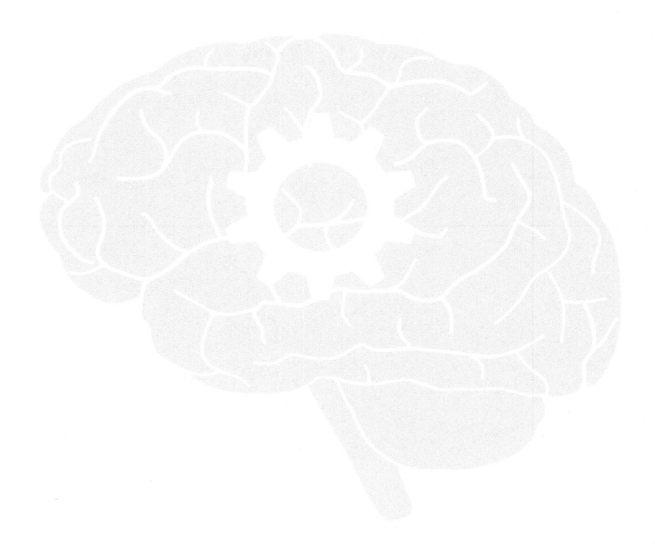

Tool 4

GRATITUDE SPIES

✳ **Purpose:** Increase gratitude awareness

👤 **User(s):** Leaders, teachers, students

 Leader Resource:

> *Building Brilliant Schools* by Dr. Andy Parker (2021), Chapters 1, 2, and 4

 Supplies:

> Worksheet G.4, Gratitude Clues

Description:

Turn your students and colleagues into gratitude spies. When we catch the gratitude passion, we begin to notice examples of and occasions for gratitude all around us. Challenge everyone in the school community to be on the lookout in the wider world for examples of gratitude, as well.

This tool focuses on noticing, identifying, and thinking about expressions of gratitude by others. In a world that is so full of difficult news and too many examples of just plain bad behavior, it is so uplifting for students to be in the habit of noticing caring, giving behaviors!

Steps:

1. Provide copies of **Worksheet G.4, Gratitude Clues**. Give these instructions:

   - Gather instances that you see or hear around the school. You can also include real examples that you hear on the news or notice in your home or public places.

   - Watch for acts of kindness, selflessness, surprising goodness, helpfulness, encouragement, advocacy, support, giving, sacrifice, or other situations that spark expressions of gratitude. Make notes about these on your Gratitude Clues sheet.

2. Provide time for gratitude spies to report, share, and discuss their clues.

   - Bring these stories to school. Share them with others—in classes, in teams, in professional development settings, or in faculty meetings. Use them as inspiration for class discussions or writing activities.

   - Teachers, be sure to share your own stories with your students—things that happen to you, others you know, or strangers. This lets them know that you, too, are aware of acts of gratitude around you.

Name _____

Gratitude Clues

Be on the lookout for gratitude

Capture some clues:

What was the clue?

What did you see or hear?

What did someone say?

What did someone do?

Where did this happen?

When did this happen?

Who showed gratitude?

Who was the receiver?

Detectives Notebook

CLUE _____

_____

_____

CLUE _____

_____

CLUE _____

_____

CLUE _____

_____

CLUE _____

_____

CLUE _____

_____

GRATITUDE

Tool 5   GRATITUDE JOURNALS

 Purpose: Increase gratitude awareness and private expression of gratitude

 User(s): Leaders, teachers, students

Leader Resource:

Building Brilliant Schools by Dr. Andy Parker (2021), Chapters 1, 2, and 4

Supplies:

Worksheet G.5, Gratitude Journal Practice

Individual notebooks for students

OR, supplies for students to make their own journals

Description:

The practice of keeping a personal gratitude journal has proven to be a highly effective intervention promoting growth in noticing, feeling, expressing, and acting on gratitude. There are many forms of journals and many ways to use them in a school setting.

This tool provides leaders, teachers, and students some suggestions for setting up a gratitude-journal process, as well as some ideas for when and what to include in gratitude journals.

Steps:

1. Leaders or teachers, make the first gratitude journal entries your own. Get in the habit of noting your own gratitude observations or experiences before asking students to start.

2. Be sure that you have an adequate supply of journals for students. They can make their own—you'll just need some paper, staples or a paper punch and rings, and perhaps posterboard for covers (and maybe a supply of fabric and/or stickers for decoration).

3. Set aside a specific time and place during the school day or class time (Examples: beginning of the day, first period, advisory period, end of day, just before lunch). This needs to be consistent. Decide if this will be daily or twice a week or other time. If this is a school-wide practice or a grade-level or team practice, you'll need to arrange that with others.

4. Plan ahead for adequate time for students to reflect as well as write.

5. Before beginning journal-keeping with students, talk with them about the process. For example, tell them they can journal about moments or instances that left them feeling grateful. They can include situations they witnessed that did not even include themselves. They can think about gratitude connected to people, situations, actions, or events. (This could be a circumstance—such as feeling safe at school or having a dog.) Encourage them to identify the benefactor, the situation, and their feelings about what they've received.

   Let students know that their statements of gratitude can be sentences, phrases, a list of phrases, paragraphs, poems, etc.

   You might suggest such starters as *I am grateful for _____ ; I am grateful to _____ for _____ ; When this happened: _____ , I was grateful; I am thankful for _____ because _____ I noticed this: _____.*

6. Use **Worksheet G.5, Gratitude Journal Practice**, for a practice run at journal entries. Students can also use this sheet as a place to collect ideas they think of or hear and keep it as a reference in the future when they write in their journals. They can add to this over time.

7. Be sure to let students know that their journals are private. Always make sharing optional.

8. Periodically, give students time to "mine" their journals for their grateful moments. During these visits to their journals, they can select something to share, if they wish.

   Author's note: As the administrator, I didn't supervise the efforts of the individual teachers and classes. But I had ongoing, consistent feedback that teachers loved how closing out the day with gratitude journaling put everyone in a more positive frame of mind. (They were thrilled that adults and kids left at the end of the day in an upbeat, grateful mood.) Students commented how it made them slow down and be more appreciative—even at home.

   I'm thankful to my staff for inspiring this practice in our school. It was such a gratifying, growth-producing experience for me personally. I kept the same journaling schedule as the students. This gave me structure—focused me to think and write. It affected my attitude, putting me into a daily mindset of valuing every encounter I had with students, staff, family, friends.

Name _____

Gratitude Journal Practice

1. Clear all distractions from your desk (and your mind).

2. Date a fresh page in your journal with today's date and time.

3. Reflect back on your day (or on your day so far, or on the past few days).

4. Capture a moment that triggered your gratitude. Think about people, actions, situations, circumstances, insights you had, things you learned about yourself or someone else, something you survived or handled, something that pleasantly surprised you, a moment of feeling valued or respected.

5. Write a sentence, phrase, group of phrases, paragraph, or other record to describe the gratitude and what sparked it.

6. Consider a response: Is there something you'd like to do in response to this gratitude you feel? If so, describe that briefly.

7. Practice writing a journal entry for today.

Journal Entry   Date _____ Time _____

Tool 6 PUTTING IT INTO WORDS

✳ **Purpose:** Practice expressing gratitude to others in a variety of ways

👤 **User(s):** Leaders, teachers, students, parents

📚 **Leader Resource:**

Building Brilliant Schools by Dr. Andy Parker, (2021), Chapters 1, 2, and 4

📝 **Supplies:**

Worksheet G.6a, Words of Gratitude: Gratitude Jar and Gratitude Phone
Worksheet G.6b, Gratitude Grams
Worksheet G.6c, Letters or Messages of Gratitude
Wide-mouth jar, paper strips, pens or markers (for Gratitude Jars)
Old-fashioned telephone and recording device (optional) (for Gratitude Pone)
Stationery or other writing paper, pens (for Gratitude Letters)
Digital devices—phones, tablets (for Digital Gratitude Messages)

Description:

The earlier tools focused on recognizing and naming, for ourselves, benefits for which we are grateful; identifying the sources of benefits; and making personal notations or descriptions of the events and our gratitude for them.

The components of this tool turn the expression outward. This encourages everyone in the school community to take the next step and express gratitude publicly or directly to the benefactor (the gift-giver who inspired the gratitude). Each strategy in this group offers a hands-on way to write, speak, and otherwise put their gratitude into words.

Steps, Gratitude Jars

This is a school-wide practice to motivate expressions of gratitude. These are shared over the intercom along with (or separate from) other announcements

1. Find a large glass jar. (Think of the Mason jars stocked in your pantry.) Decorate and label it.

2. Place the jar in any visible, high-traffic place. (Think office, cafeteria, hallway, lobby, classroom, media center.) See **Worksheet G.6a, Words of Gratitude**.

3. Next to the jar, place a box with slips of paper and a pen.

4. Anyone in the school can anonymously write gratitude statements and place them in the jar.

5. On a regular basis, read some statements from the jar.

Steps, Gratitude Phone:

The Gratitude Phone is a tool for younger students to use to express gratitude. Use an "old-fashioned" desk phone, or other land-line type of phone. If it is possible to set up a recording device near the phone, students can record their gratitude messages. Even without capturing the messages, it is good practice for students to speak their expressions of thanks.

1. Set up the phone. Demonstrate use of the phone for the students.

2. Take turns practicing speaking the messages.

3. Remind students to include the "Who" and "What." See Worksheet **G.6a, Words of Gratitude**.

Steps, Gratitude Gram:

You might have to teach your students (and maybe some of your colleagues) about the "gram" idea—back to the old telegrams. The Gratitude Grams are short, but specific, expressions of gratitude that tell what happened and who was behind it—along with thankfulness.

1. Discuss the "gram" idea with students. Some may be familiar with candy grams! Use **Worksheet G.6b, Gratitude Grams**, as a guide and as a place to practice. But students will love to create and decorate their own. They may want to add a small lollipop or other candy!

2. Students can decide how they want to deliver the grams.
   Author's Note: These can be used as a school fundraiser. One of my schools used grams designed in their graphics design class for a professional look. Grams were sold for a small price to members of the school and wider community. Buyers completed the grams. The school set up a system for distributing them within the school community.

Steps, Letters or Messages of Gratitude:

Writing a gratitude letter is a powerful way to deepen benefits for the senders and receivers.

1. Encourage students to write a letter or digital message to someone who did something that has inspired their gratitude. You might suggest that they choose someone who has not yet been adequately thanked for the action.

2. Writers can follow the suggestions on **Worksheet G.6c, Letters or Messages of Gratitude**.

Name _____

Words of Gratitude

Gratitude Jar

1. Write a statement of something or someone for which you are grateful in your class or the school. Be sure to mention the action.

2. Sign your name if you wish.

3. Put the note in the jar.

Jenna Adams and her friends rescued me when I got stuck at the top of the monkey bars.

I'm grateful for today's fire drill. It helps me feel safe.

I appreciate the principal's funny jokes during morning announcements.

Soban gave me a pencil—twice. That was nice.

I liked that Mario helped me clean up the mess after art class.

Ashanti shared her cookie with me. She didn't have to do that.

Thank you Ms. Brett, for helping me understand the math today.

Gratitude Phone

1. Pick up the phone.

2. Push the button.

3. Talk into the phone. Tell about something that you are thankful for.

4. If it includes a person, tell what that person did.

5. Hang up the phone.

Name _____

Gratitude Grams

What is a gram?

A gram is a form of some sort that gives a short, important message with words, drawings, or both. You've probably heard of a telegram, a candy-gram, a diagram, or an Instagram!

What is a gratitude gram?

A gratitude gram is a message of gratitude. (Sometimes people add candy when the gratitude gram is delivered!) You can design a gratitude gram however you like. Just remember to:

- Keep it short.

- Be specific about why you are thankful.

- Say what's important.

- Include the name of the recipient.

- Include the recipient's address (or class, room number, etc.).

- Include the sender's name and the date.

Use this as a model for your gram. Then cut it out and deliver it!

Date	**Gratitude Gram**	School

Recipient _____ Room Number or Class _____

Message:

_____

_____

_____

_____

_____

_____

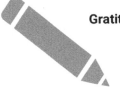

Name _____

Letters or Messages of Gratitude

Use this page to collect your ideas for writing a letter, note, or digital message responding to someone about something that inspired your gratitude. After you've gathered your thoughts, get some stationery or your device and write your letter!

Thoughts and Notes

_____
_____
_____
_____
_____
_____
_____
_____
_____
_____
_____
_____
_____
_____
_____
_____

Writing Gratitude Letters and Messages

• Choose one experience or situation.

• Think about the person or persons who did or gave something without expecting anything in return.

• Identify what the action was.

• Think about how you want to express your gratitude.

• Address the letter to that person.

• Write your thoughts to express gratitude. Be specific about what was done.

• Be specific about how that helped, inspired, or otherwise affected you.

• Be specific about how you felt about the situation.

• Decide if you will give the letter to the person, mail it, read it to the person, or something else. It's up to you to choose what you do with it.

• Pay attention to your own experience of writing the letter. How does this feel? What did you learn?

Tool 7

THE ART OF GRATITUDE

✳ **Purpose:** Provide a variety of ways (and media) through which to express gratitude or to show its effects or benefits

👤 **User(s):** Leaders, teachers, students

📚 **Leader Resource:**

Building Brilliant Schools by Dr. Andy Parker (2021), Chapters 1, 2, and 4

📝 **Supplies:**

Worksheet G.7, Gratitude Art Plan

Posterboard or paper for collecting brainstormed ideas

Markers

Materials as needed for individual art choices

Description:

Gratitude does not have to be expressed in words alone. There are many forms of expression that are useful for communicating or reflecting on gratitude. Arts, including visual and performing arts, are powerful tools for communicating gratitude or identifying benefits that have been received.

This tool inspires students to tap into their gratitude and to "think beyond the spoken or written words" for showing or sharing it.

Steps:

1. Say to students: *Close your eyes. Think of something you feel grateful about. Visualize gratitude. Tap into how it feels inside. What colors or shapes or movements come to your mind? What rhythms or tunes come to your mind? How would you show your gratitude for something or describe benefits you have received from someone if you could not use the usual methods of telling them or writing a letter or note?*

   What could you create, design, or demonstrate to depict gratitude?

2. Give them a few quiet minutes to ponder this.

3. Allow for a good brainstorming session. Participants can do this in pairs, then have pairs share with other pairs, then combine ideas with the whole class—or just have a lively, whole-class idea-gathering session!

4. Have a "scribe" or two ready to jot down the ideas as the group brainstorms.

   You, the teacher or leader, can certainly contribute ideas as well—but let students take the strongest lead. Here are a few ideas:

   - posters or collages of all kinds, including with "found" words and images
   - chalk designs (no drawings—just expressing with color and lines and flow)
   - light shows or shadow shows
   - paintings
   - drawings or diagrams
   - sculptures with string or wire or other media
   - photo journals
   - dances
   - mimes
   - rhymes
   - rhythms and raps
   - songs
   - poems
   - visual anagram
   - videos

5. Distribute copies of **Worksheet G.7, Gratitude Art Plan**, for students to begin planning or thinking about something they'd like to create artistically to explain or express gratitude or to show the one or more benefits they have received

6. Then . . . be sure to provide materials, a process, time, and space for students or staff to create, and then to show, share, explain, perform their gratitude art. If students choose, they may wish to do this with an audience of the people to whom they are grateful.

Name _____

Gratitude Art Plan

Use this guide to plan your artistic explanation or expression of gratitude.

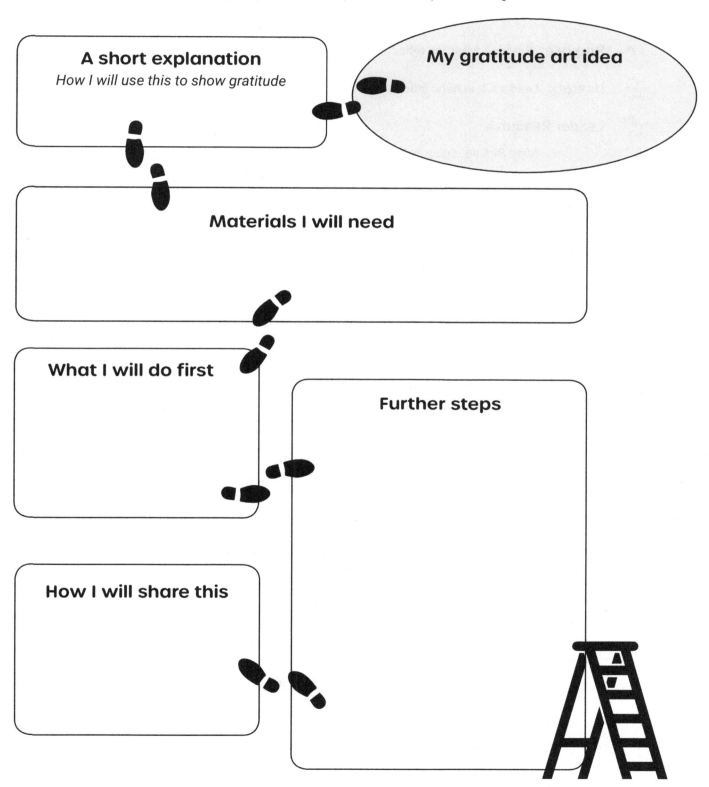

A short explanation
How I will use this to show gratitude

My gratitude art idea

Materials I will need

What I will do first

Further steps

How I will share this

Tool 8   GRATITUDE CIRCLES

✷ **Purpose:** Practice gratitude reflection, analysis, and expression

👤 **User(s):** Leaders, teachers, students

📚 **Leader Resource:**

Building Brilliant Schools by Dr. Andy Parker, (2021), Chapters 1, 2, and 4

📝 **Supplies:**

Worksheet G.8, Gratitude Circle Guidelines
Posterboard or poster paper
Compass or circle pattern
Markers

Description:

A gratitude circle is a warm and wonderful way to close out any period of time that a group has spent together. Think of this as you meet with your faculty for the last time of the year, as you say goodbye to your students for the school year (or before a holiday break), as your team completes a major project. It's a moving and fulfilling strategy for any farewell or milestone.

This tool gives students or adults a way to reflect on a period of time spent with a group of others—in particular, to remember what interactions, actions, or circumstances inspire their gratitude. And then, they get a good chance to express that gratitude directly.

Steps:

1. Read through the following steps for gratitude circles. (See 3 below.) Consider the process or protocols that are important for your group or class.

2. Create a poster that can be posted to guide groups as they use a gratitude circle. **Worksheet G.8, Gratitude Circle Guidelines**, provides a blank template. You can design your own, or after holding a gratitude circle, give students the task of designing and creating the poster. As an alternative to one large circle poster, individual guidelines could be written (by small groups) on circles posted together or around the room. (See examples on page 41.)

3. When it is time for the circle:

- The participants should have some advance notice and some time to think. Give a preparation instruction such as: *Think of something that happened or was given to you during the year (class, semester, project, etc.) for which you can thank someone.*

- Gather in a circle. Take turns speaking, but not necessarily in any order. People can speak if they wish.

- If this is a setting with a teacher and students, the teacher can go first to model the process.

- Avoid general statements such as: *Thank you for being nice,* or *Thank you for being a good friend (helper, team member, colleague),* or *I'm grateful you worked on that report with me.*

- Be specific. Say what happened. Explain precisely what you appreciated: *Thank you for being "my right arm" when I broke my arm. You put my backpack on and off my back every day, and unloaded and loaded my books.*

- Tell the person what the gesture or action did for you or how you felt in response to it: *It took away my worries about getting along with one arm that didn't work. Every day, I was comfortable and cheerful coming to school, because I knew you would be there to help me.*

- Make sure every person in the group is thanked for something.

Name _____

Gratitude Circle Guidelines

Use this circle to display guidelines your group will follow in the use of Gratitude Circles. Then cut out the circle and back it with cardboard, posterboard, wood, foam core, or other sturdy material. Display the guidelines in a prominent place.

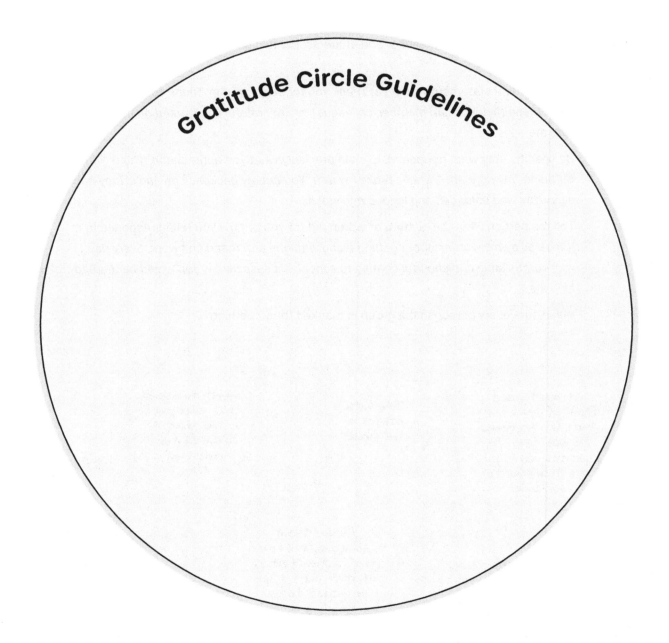

Tool 9 GRATITUDE RISK-BENEFIT PRACTICE

⊛ **Purpose:** Provide practice in analysis of gratitude experiences

🧍 **User(s):** Leaders, teachers, students

📚 **Leader Resource:**

Building Brilliant Schools by Dr. Andy Parker (2021), Chapters 1, 2, and 4

📝 **Supplies:**

Worksheet G.9, Risk-Benefit Appraisal

Description:

A 2014 study with children ages 8 to 11 showed that young people could be trained to think gratefully (Froh et al.). Classes were randomly assigned to weekly activities in a control group or in what was called "the benefit-appraisal curriculum" group. The benefits-appraisal curriculum included discussions, role-playing activities, and writing assignments designed to teach students to appraise (examine and evaluate) grateful thoughts and actions. Within just a few days, researchers saw increases in benefit appraisal skills, in grateful mood, and in behavioral evidences of gratitude (as compared to the control group). A follow-up study of weekly sessions over five weeks also showed increase in students' appraisals of benefits of grateful thinking. In addition, researchers found increases in positive mood, students' positive affect (well-being), general life satisfaction, and a number of outward expressions of gratitude. Furthermore, these benefits were still in effect five months after the experiment.

This tool guides practice in benefit appraisal. It is a great set of skills for all ages—and especially for adults in a school community! These skills deepen and expand understandings and expressions of gratitude beyond the habit of a quick "Thank you."

Steps with Adults:

1. Start the process of risk-benefit appraisal by practicing it with colleagues. Adults will do a better job of leading this with students if they have experienced it themselves. Teachers can discuss the process and share advice or ideas on how to make it work well for their students.

2. Gather or invent scenarios in which someone helped someone else—or otherwise provided a benefit for someone else. Begin with adult scenarios. In the study mentioned above (Froh, et al., 2014), the appraisals began with hypothetical scenarios. Students were asked to imagine themselves as the main character in a story. Then they were asked to answer four questions, with answer choices ranging from 1 to 5 (or not at all to totally). The questions were:

   How much did the person help you on purpose?
   Ratings ranged from not at all to slightly to extremely.

   How much did the person give up to help you?
   Ratings ranged from nothing to a great deal.

   How much did that actually help you?
   Ratings ranged from not at all to somewhat to a great deal.

   How thankful did you feel toward the benefactor?
   Ratings ranged from not at all to totally.

3. Work in your team, faculty group, grade-level group, or other group to listen to some scenarios, imagine yourselves as the main character, and respond to those questions with a rating of 1 to 5. Discuss your outcomes.

4. Use **Worksheet G.9, Risk-Benefit Appraisal**, to practice using a scenario where YOU have been the recipient. Discuss your outcomes if you wish.

Steps with Students:

1. Follow a similar process as above. With students, you might choose to stay with hypothetical scenarios once a week for a few weeks before moving to the personal experiences. They can use **Worksheet G.9, Risk-Benefit Appraisal**, for either imagined or real situations.

2. Give students time to discuss the process. They can talk about what they learned, what questions arose, or how easy it was to answer the questions. Ask them to reflect, also, on how doing this appraisal affects their own experiences as both a benefactor and receiver.

Note: Benefit appraisal can be done with any age. Keep to topics that are age-appropriate and not too emotionally charged. Adapt the discussions to the age level. Invite students to suggest situations or create stories. Do be sure to continue practicing this with colleagues:

Name _____

Risk-Benefit Appraisal

Choose a situation or scenario in which gratitude has been expressed. This guide will help you take a deeper look at the grateful actions or attitudes that someone has given to or directed at you or others.

Who was the benefactor?

Who was the receiver?

What happened? For what was the receiver grateful?

INTENT: Was this act done on purpose? Somewhat on purpose? Not at all on purpose?

COST: What did the benefactor give up or risk to do this?

BENEFIT(s): What were benefits to the receiver?

EFFECT(s): How did the receiver feel in response? What did the receiver think, say, or do?

Tool 10 REFLECTING ON THE TOOLS

✳ Purpose: Examine personal experience working with the tools in this Gratitude pillar

👤 User(s): Leaders, teachers, (students, optional)

📚 Leader Resource:

Building Brilliant Schools by Dr. Andy Parker, (2021), Chapters 1 through 4

📝 Supplies:

Worksheet G.10, Looking Back and Looking Forward
A list of the tools that have been used from this chapter
Results of completed tasks from tools in this chapter

Description:

This tool offers a way for those who have used the tools in this section to reflect on what they have done and learned. In addition, it inspires a look forward as to what concepts, behaviors, or goals they will develop and use in the future.

Steps:

1. Distribute copies of **Worksheet G.10, Looking Back and Looking Forward,** as a guide. Also provide a list of the tools that have been used by individuals or groups in their work together. In addition, if the folks reflecting have saved any products or worksheets from the individual tools—these would be helpful to have on hand as participants reflect over their experiences.

2. With the worksheet as a guide, individuals reflect on their own and note their reflections. If students have used some of the tools, you might invite them to do the same or similar process of reflection.

3. Depending on the setting, groups may choose to share and discuss their reflections. Teams or grade-level groups or entire faculties may wish to use the reflections to set goals together.

Looking Back and Looking Forward

Reflect on what you learned, thought, experienced, and wish to do further with the tools in this pillar. Write a comment in each category.

Most powerful tool for me, and why	
Most challenging tool for me, and why	
A key idea I learned	
Tool that I think will be great for my students, and why	
Tool that's been most helpful to my group of colleagues, and why	
Something I learned about myself while using these tools	
Two goals I want to set for myself related to the tools in this pillar	

Chapter 2

Tools for Your RELATIONSHIPS Toolbox

The central element in promoting learning is promoting relationships.
— **Charles Leadbeater, Author, Management Advisor**

This collection of tools focuses on the researched-based traits, skills, or practices that have been identified as key influences on the development of gratitude and on the numerous benefits that follow from regular gratitude practice.

⚙ Definitions

Relationship:
> *a connection with oneself or with another person or group of persons that is based on positive bonds—a connection that is respectful, caring, and trusting; a connection that is trustworthy—something one can count on*

Self-Awareness:
> *a key component of one's relationship with oneself, this is having insight and understanding of personal values, feelings, motives, moods, intentions, drives, and emotional triggers and responses—as well as noticing and understanding the effects of these personal characteristics and responses on others*

⚙ Key Benefits of High-Quality Adult-Student Relationships
For the students . . .

(Includes student relationships with teachers and other adults in the school community)

- Increased academic performance and academic resilience
- Higher levels of motivation and engagement
- Greater feelings of safety and security
- Increased prosocial skills and behavior
- Greater sense of school belonging
- Enhanced autonomy, self-direction, self-confidence, and self-esteem
- Increased academic tenacity
- Reduced anxiety, stress, isolation, withdrawal, and depression
- Increase in overall school adjustment, satisfaction, and connection

- More satisfying, trusting relationships among peers

- Higher attendance and lower dropout rates

- Diminished negative behaviors toward others

- Protection against long-term internalization of negative internal behaviors

- Positive impact on long-term success in school and employment

- Buffering effect in the presence of bullying and distress in students' lives.

- Some protection against the consequences of even the worst psychological trauma

For the adults . . .

(Includes relationships with students, parents, and colleagues—including leaders)

- Higher self-efficacy (belief in ability to do their job well)

- Less job stress

- Higher job satisfaction and higher job performance

- Greater feelings of support and comfort in their jobs

- Higher general sense of connection to the school community

- Higher rates of cooperation and comradery

- Higher trust in school leadership and other colleagues

- Greater sense of being valued

- More satisfaction that they know their students

- Better communication with colleagues and parents

- Greater success with classroom management; fewer behavioral disruptions in the classroom

- More willingness to take risks, to learn and grow, and to engage in new practices and programs

- Greater creativity in teaching

- Experience of more joy in their students and their jobs

⚙ Key Benefits of High-Quality Student Peer Relationships

Peers can provide or enhance for one another . . .

- Models for engagement and success in learning activities

- Academic challenge and academic risk taking

- A sense of belonging that is separate from families

- Emotional and social support and connections at school

- Help to shape prosocial behavior

- Opportunities to learn appropriate social interactions

- Models and motivation for self-management

- Help for crossing barriers and adjusting to school

- Protection against stress

- Models of willingness to help

- Situations for learning and honing such skills and behaviors as caring, empathy, communication, cooperation, compromise, social responsibility, negotiation, conflict resolution, and problem-solving

- Self-awareness, self-confidence, and self-esteem

- Self-direction and independence

- Awareness of others' needs, values, and perspectives

Note: For a more complete discussion of definitions and benefits of quality relationships, as well as consequences of missing, strained, or toxic relationships; and for information about interventions to improve relationships, see Chapters 5 through 7 in *Building Brilliant Schools: What G.R.E.A.T. Leaders Do Differently*, by Dr. Andy Parker (2021).

Use the next page to keep notes from your reading of those chapters.

⚙ Relationships Tools for Brilliant Schools

11. Comings and Goings (Teacher-Student Relationships; Leader-Staff Relationships)

12. Say My Name, Say My Name (Teacher-Student Relationships; Peer Relationships)

13. Getting-to-Know-You Bingo (Getting to Know Each Other; Any School Relationships)

14. Write Me a Letter (Teacher-Student, Teacher-Parent, Colleague-Colleague Relationships)

15. Relationship Inspection (Teacher-Student Relationship; Other School Relationships)

16. Sparking Class Connections (Class Relationships and Unity)

17. Relationship Selfies (Peer Relationships)

18. Perspective-Taking (Peer Relationships; Other School Relationships)

19. Family Connections (School-Home Relationships)

20. Reflecting on the Tools (Self-evaluation of Use of Relationship Tools)

Notes from Relationships Chapters

Building Brilliant Schools: What G.R.E.A.T. Leaders Do Differently, Chapters 5–7

As you read about Relationships, jot down key ideas or points that you want to remember from each chapter.

Chapter 5, What Are Relationships?

Chapter 6, Why Relationships?

    Self-Awareness

    Teacher-Student Relationships

    Other Adult-Student Relationships

    Student-Student Relationships

    Adult-Adult Relationships

    Role of Leaders

Chapter 7, How Do G.R.E.A.T. Leaders Get Results with Relationships?

Tool 11 COMINGS AND GOINGS

 Purpose: Build and sustain teacher-student relationships (or leader-student or colleague-colleague relationships) by being present and communicative when school, classes, meetings, or other gatherings begin and end

 User(s): Leaders, teachers

Leader Resource:

Building Brilliant Schools by Dr. Andy Parker (2021), Chapters 5 through 7

Supplies:

Worksheet R.11, Beginnings and Endings Checklist

Description:

Okay, this may seem like a no-brainer. You've heard it before: "Give a personal greeting to everyone who enters your classroom—every day!" "Always say goodbye as students leave your classroom—every day!" You probably do a lot of this already. But, how many mornings are you in a hurry, stressed, running behind, trying to get everything ready—that you don't step in the hallway or the doorway to greet students? Or, if you have several classes in a row, how many times do you not make it to the doorway at the beginning of each class? And how often does a day or class end and you're so focused on one person, issue, or last instruction to students—that you send them off without everyone hearing a goodbye?

Relationships start before the morning bell rings and continue after the final bell of the day! This tool gives teachers or leaders a way to keep the importance of beginnings and endings at the forefront of their minds and behaviors.

Steps:

1. Make a commitment to being there, making some sort of brief contact—with every student or member of the gathering, when they arrive and before they leave—every time. Surely, there will be times when it just can't be done. But on as regular a basis as absolutely possible . . .

   • Get away from your desk or last-minute preparations and get to the door.

   • SEE each student who enters the door. Greet each by name in a way that lets all students know you are glad to see them arrive in your room.

   • LOOK in the person's eyes. You can get an immediate "read" on each student. You can notice how their day is going, and how they feel about entering your class.

- This moment—just a second or two—gives you a chance to give a word or smile of encouragement that may make all the difference in how the class period (or the whole day) goes for that student.

- At the end of class, try to have all your tasks and announcements finished before that bell rings. Be at the door again as students leave.

- Give a cheerful, positive sendoff and a fun goodbye for everyone to hear.

- As much as possible, let each student know that he or she is noticed as you say goodbye. If you have a class handshake or signal, engage each student this way also.

2. Use Worksheet **R.11, Beginnings and Endings Checklist**, as a tool to maintain consistency in your presence and contact as students arrive and leave. Do a quick scan through it and make checkmarks. Don't let the check-up take much time from actually **connecting** with students. Use the worksheet for at least two weeks. Hopefully you'll build the habit! Then come back to the worksheet once a month or so for a quick re-check. Enlist students to help you remember.

3. Think beyond the "regular" classroom scenario.

- **Do not limit this to students.** Every day, find moments to greet fellow staff members. Start the day off letting colleagues know you are happy to see them and work with them. Wish them a good day. Wish them a connective farewell when you can.

- **Spread greetings and farewells to parents.** Don't miss an opportunity to pass a cheerful greeting, if only a wave or a smile, to any parents you see on your way into the building or through the halls.

- **Leaders:** This is a must for you! Do not be in your office hiding away or doing "important" business when staff members, students, or parents arrive. Greet as many as you possibly can. Make a quick round past classrooms, through the cafeteria, into the gym, or wherever staff members are in the morning. Be outside to smile and wave at parents dropping off students. Give a positive welcome to students. Be around at the end of the day to send people off with your care.

Beginnings and Endings Checklist

Scan this list of good beginning-and-ending behaviors. Each day for two weeks, do a quick self-check as to how you did on this. Mark ✔ if you're satisfied with how you did. Write **N** if you know you need to step up with one.

	M	T	W	Th	F	M	T	W	Th	F
I was at the door or in the hall before the first class member arrived.										
I greeted each student by name.										
I greeted students in a way that showed I was glad to see them arrive.										
In these moments, I was able to get some clues as to the mood of some students.										
I ended class with enough time for ending comments and sendoff.										
We all had a cheerful sendoff phrase or moment.										
I was at the door or in a place where I could say farewell to students.										
I feel that all or most students felt noticed as they left.										

Tool 12   SAY MY NAME, SAY MY NAME

✳ **Purpose:** Build relationships by honoring the names and correct pronunciation of names of each student and others in the school community

👤 **User(s):** Leaders, teachers, students

📚 **Leader Resource:**

Building Brilliant Schools by Dr. Andy Parker, (2021), Chapters 5 through 7

📝 **Supplies:**

Worksheet R.12, About My Name
Art supplies as needed for any "Name Art" project chosen

Description:

"Names have power." —Rick Riordan, author of *The Lightning Thief*

This strategy is for everyone in the school. It starts with leaders, teachers, and all staff. But get students in on it too! The tool suggests a way to learn the correct pronunciation for each name and to find out what the person wants to be called. Yes, this is a fairly simple strategy. But it is no small matter! It is a momentous way to show respect, care, and connection.

Steps:

1. Use a few small moments at the beginning of the school year to connect with students around their names. This takes minimal effort and yields big rewards. Let students know that you want to know their names and how to say them. You can begin by saying something like this: "Help me say your name correctly, okay? I mess up names all the time, so please be patient with me. I will work to get it right, but I might need you to coach me and to remind me. Okay? Your name is part of who you are. I respect you, so I want to get it right."

2. Use **Worksheet R.12, About My Name**, as a way for them to let you know their names, by what name they want to be called, and how to pronounce the names. This sheet can substitute for one-on-one conversations, which might take too long. Give a little lesson on some clear ways they can write a name phonetically (e.g., Charlene = *shar + lean* or Jorge = *hor-hay*). When they are finished, they can cut it into a card-sized paper and give it to the teacher.

3. Then, work hard to practice the names, and use the names when you see the students.

4. For the final question on the "name card," students might comment on what they know about the origin of their name (if anything) or the reason why their parents (or they) chose that name or nickname.

5. Follow the same advice with students' parents and with colleagues. Find out what they want you to call them and how to pronounce it correctly.

6. Make sure that students also learn the names that their peers choose to use in the classroom. Give students time to practice correct pronunciation of each other's' names, as well.

7. Remember to follow steps 1-6 with any new students that enter your class during the year.

8. Early in the year, allow time for students to do some Name Art. This is a cool way to build self-esteem and pride in one's name. Brainstorm art ideas with students. One idea that can get them started is to make a colorful design with their name (first, last, nickname—whatever they choose). They

   • Draw the letters, in a large size, in a design to fill a large piece of drawing paper. The idea is the that the letters can be in any position and any arrangement that takes the lines all the way to the edges of the paper and that touch other letters in at least one spot. When the name is written (in marker), it divides the paper into interesting shapes.

   • Fill the shapes with colors, designs, stripes, or any patterns to make a visually-fun image to show off the name.

This is just one approach to a name design. Encourage other ideas—collages, paintings, posters, mobiles, videos, sculptures—anything that visually shows off their names.

About My Name

✂ Write the information about your name. Cut out the card. Give it to the teacher.

Please, say my name right!

Write your name as it is on your school records.

_____

Help me say it correctly. Write the way it sounds.

_____

What name would you like me to use when I speak to you, call on you, or write your name in this class? (a nickname?)

_____

Help me say this correctly. Write it the way it sounds.

_____

Is there anything else you want to tell me about your name?

_____

Choose or add an idea to represent your name with visual art. Let the teacher know what supplies you need.
Here are a few ideas: collage (with cut-out words, pictures, or found objects)
colorful chalk or marker design
crayon mosaic
painting
sculpture

Tool 13   GETTING-TO-KNOW-YOU BINGO

Purpose: Start the process of helping group members begin to learn some things about each other—as a beginning step to building connections, respect, and relationships

User(s): Leaders, teachers, students

Leader Resource:

Building Brilliant Schools by Dr. Andy Parker (2021), Chapters 5 through 7

Supplies:

Worksheet R.13a, Find Someone Who . . . Bingo (Template)
Worksheet R.13b, Find Someone Who . . . Bingo (Sample for Students)
Worksheet R.13c, Find Someone Who . . . Bingo (Sample for Adults)
Pencils or pens

Description:

Relationships begin with knowing each other. The more a person knows another as a human being with skills, ideas, experiences, and feelings, the easier it will be to learn and get along with that person. A good way to get to know students or colleagues is to inspire them to tell you about themselves. There are dozens of ways to do this. Many teachers do an activity where students complete sentences or phrases to identify traits about themselves. However, many of the usual "icebreakers" require students to take uncomfortable risks and share personal information with people they barely know.

This tool (and some other alternatives suggested later) get people interacting on topics that are personal but not too sensitive. It's a strategy that provides a non-threatening way to learn a bit about each other without the discomfort of being asked to share too much that is deeply personal. Save those kinds of activities for later in your time together as a group.

Steps:

1. Give instructions to the group: Tell students that you'll be giving them a BINGO board (sheet) with 24 short descriptions. They are to find someone in the group who will agree that they fit the description. That person will autograph the sheet with initials.

2. Let students know that they may need to use one person twice, but the goal is to get signatures from as many different people as possible—hopefully, almost everyone in the group. If they don't know the person's name, they should be sure to ask for the first and last name.

3. Distribute copies of **Worksheet R.13b, Find Someone Who . . . Bingo**, to students. Make sure everyone has a working pen or pencil for autographs. If your BINGO board has a blank space in the center, students may add an idea of their own. (As an alternative to Worksheet R.13b, use **Worksheet R.13a, BINGO Template**, for yourself or your students to create your own BINGO game.) In an adult learning setting, use **Worksheet R.13c** as a model for a BINGO game.

4. Set a timer for 10-15 minutes for this activity (vary this as needed).

5. Ask students to return to their seats and add a checkmark or their own initials to the descriptions that are true of themselves! Take some time for them to be able to note which students share similar characteristics, situations, or experiences with them. This is an important part of the process.

6. You can make a few different BINGO boards as part of the activity, so not everyone will be looking for the same things. Students of all ages will probably love to make their own BINGO boards for a second round of the activity.

Alternative for all ages:

- **BINGO Variations.** Make the task more of a traditional BINGO game—where they try to get autographs to complete a row (or 2, 3, etc.) This makes the activity shorter.

- **Circle Up!** Form two concentric circles—one inside the other. The outside circle will have wider spaces between people. Each student on the outside circle faces a student on the inside circle. Ask such questions as, *How did you get to school this morning?* Or *What is the most exciting adventure you have had or hope to have? OR Who is your favorite musical artist?* Give a minute or two for the answers. Facing people each answer the question. Then the outside circle moves one person to the right before another question is asked. This activity works great with "Would You Rather" questions (e.g., *Would you rather write a paragraph or solve a tricky math word problem? Why? OR Would you rather sing in front of a group or dance in front of a group? Why? Would you rather be invisible or be able to speak five languages? Why?*)

Find Someone Who . . . BINGO

For each square, get a signature (initials) of someone who fits the description.

B	I	N	G	O
		You write this description!		

Find Someone Who . . . BINGO

For each square, get a signature (initials) of someone who fits the description.

BINGO

Has the same birthday month as you	Has had a cavity fixed by a dentist	Ate ice cream this week	Lives near their grandparents	Wants to go to college
Has a sibling in this school	Is not afraid of spiders	Wants to start a business	Walked to school today	Can ride a skateboard
Has been out of the country	Can curl their tongue	You write this description!	Has been in a parade	Loves to draw, paint, or build things
Is a twin or has twin siblings	Can speak two languages	Has the same number of pets as you	Has the same place in family as you (only child, oldest, youngest, etc.)	Likes to perform music
Will show you one of their favorite dances	Is wearing the same color clothing as you	Has had stitches	Lives with three other people	Has the same favorite video game as you

Name _____

Find Someone Who . . . BINGO

For each square, get a signature (initials) of someone who fits the description.

Has been in education about as long as you	Will say she or he has a great sense of humor	Has never eaten sushi	Has had more than one broken bone	Is having an especially frustrating week
Has seriously considered leaving the profession due to stress	Doesn't like chocolate	Didn't eat breakfast today	Is comfortable with a productively noisy classroom	Speaks a language you don't
Lives in an apartment	Has a great icebreaker idea for kids	You write this description!	Plays a musical instrument	Has been terrified of a student's parent
Has had a profession outside the field of education	Likes to read science fiction	Feels behind schedule with planning or grading	Is from or in a military family	Has been camping in the last year
Sings or performs in some sort of musical group	Listens to music on a turntable	Meditates regularly	Has never had a traffic or parking ticket	Is a vegan

Tool 14

WRITE ME A LETTER

✸ **Purpose:** Students introduce themselves to their teachers (or colleagues introduce themselves to one another) as an early step in getting to know one another and building relationships

👤 **User(s):** Students, teachers, leaders, parents

📖 **Leader Resource:**

Building Brilliant Schools by Dr. Andy Parker, (2021), Chapters 5 through 7

📝 **Supplies:**

Worksheet R.14a, Letter to My Teacher
Worksheet R.14b, Letter to My Child's Teacher
Worksheet R.14c, Letter to My Colleague
Stationery, posterboard, drawing supplies

Description:

Many of us don't write letters much anymore. But somehow, putting "ourselves" into a letter makes use of self-reflection skills and expression skills that don't get used quite the same way in verbal dialogue—or even in emails, texts, or artistic versions. This tool offers a process and some suggestions for students to write introductory letters to their teachers. It gives them a private way to say some things they want the teacher to know about themselves. The tool also suggests some other uses of the introductory-letter ideas.

Steps for Leaders or Leaders and Staff Together:

1. The teacher goes first. This is a way for the teacher or leader to break the ice, letting students know some things about herself or himself. The teacher can write a letter and read it. Or it could be a video letter or letter accompanied by slides. Give a little background on yourself—include something about your family and your outside interests. Don't hesitate to share such information as silly things, things important to you, your skills, some bloopers, what kind of a teacher you will be, and what your hopes or goals are for the school year.

2. Ask students to write a letter to you. You can use **Worksheet R.14a, Letter to My Teacher**, as a guide to help them plan their letters. This example gives guiding questions, but you can create your own guide that has different questions or is more open-ended. Whatever your instructions, give guidelines that allow for fairly short letters. Students can write as much as they wish, but the "assignment" must not seem overwhelming.

3. Allow some time for students to make notes about what they'll want to answer or add.

4. Supply stationery for students to write their letters. You might offer alternatives if you think it will work better for some or all students. For example, students could create a collage of statements, an audio letter, or a video letter. Or some may wish to glue the letter to posterboard and surround it with sketches, cartoons, diagrams, or other graphic elements that expand the message. Whatever the format, the final outcome should still have the spirit of a "Dear Teacher" letter and contain whatever questions or content you've initially outlined.

5. Students give their letters to the teacher—after your assurances that you will honor what they have shared and that all letters will be kept confidential.

Other good uses of letter-writing:

- Teacher-to-Family Letters: The teacher writes a short letter introducing herself or himself to families—telling what they'd like the families to know about them, their teaching goals, their enthusiasm for their students, some plans or ideas for the school year, and some appropriate personal information. Make sure this letter is translated to the language of the family, if needed.

- Parent-to-Teacher Letters: Teachers invite parents to write a letter telling what they'd like the teacher to know about their child and their family. See sample template, **Worksheet R.14b, Letter to My Child's Teacher**, for some ideas about components of such a letter. Share such a "guide" with the parents. Let parents know that they are free to write to you in the language with which they are most comfortable. Then you find a way to translate this, if needed.

- Colleague-to-Colleague Letters: Leaders, invite your teachers and other school staff members to write letters to one another. In the same spirit as the letters described above, this letter offers an opportunity for the staff member to tell a colleague (or a group of colleagues) some things they'd like others to know about themselves—as a person, as a colleague, as an educator. Engage in this process yourself. Your first letter could be to your entire staff. See sample template on **Worksheet R.14c, Letter to My Colleague** for some ideas about components of such a letter. Invite your staff members to a write letter to you, as well.

Name _____

Letter to My Teacher

Introduce yourself to the teacher by writing a letter. Answer the starred questions and at least two others in your letter. Your letter will be private.

⭐ What are the most important things you want the teacher to know about you?

⭐ What do you hope will happen for you in this class this year?

⭐ What skills or characteristics will you contribute to the class?

⭐ How do you learn best?

Is there something you hope does not happen in this class? What?

What would you like to get better at in this class?

What is something you hope the teacher will do well?

Anything else? Write anything else you want the teacher to know or any questions you would like to ask.

Use the back of this paper if you need more room.

Dear Teacher,

_____
_____
_____
_____
_____
_____
_____
_____
_____
_____
_____
_____
_____
_____
_____
_____
_____
_____

Name _____

Letter to My Child's Teacher

Introduce yourself to the teacher by writing a letter. It would be helpful if you could answer the starred questions and make any other comments you would like. Your letter will be private. Only the teacher will see it.

⭐ What are the most important things you want the teacher to know about your child?

⭐ What are your hopes or goals for your child at school this year?

⭐ What strengths does your child have that you want me to see in the classroom?

⭐ What helps your child learn best?

You could also tell something about one or more of these:

Your child's interests

Skills you want your child to improve

Your child's social skills

Your child's academic habits

What frustrates the child at school

Anything you are worried about related to school

Something you hope the teacher will do well

Anything else you want the teacher to know

Use the back of this paper if you need more room.

Dear Teacher,

Letter to My Colleague

Introduce yourself to me (or us) by writing a letter. Answer the starred questions and add any other information you wish. Your letters will be private.

⭐ What are the most important things you want me (us) to know about you?

⭐ What do you hope will happen for you or for your students at school this year?

⭐ What skills or characteristics will you contribute to this school (team, faculty, group)?

Your passions

Your teaching or learning style

Personal interests

Family information

How you relax or have fun

Professional development you'd like to see offered

Your ideas about what makes a healthy, welcoming school culture

What you need from colleagues or from school leaders

Use the back of this paper if you need more room.

Dear Colleague(s),

_____

_____

_____

_____

_____

_____

_____

_____

_____

_____

_____

_____

_____

_____

_____

_____

_____

Tool 15   RELATIONSHIP INSPECTION

 Purpose: Examine relationships with individual students; notice patterns in relationships

 User(s): Leaders, teachers

Leader Resource:

Building Brilliant Schools by Dr. Andy Parker (2021), Chapters 5 through 7

Supplies:

Worksheet R.15a, Signs of Quality Teacher-Student Relationships
Worksheet R.15b, Guide for Relationship Inspection
Worksheet R.15c, Relationship Inspection Record
Student roster for each class

Description:

Sometimes, we think we know our students from being around them all day or several times a week. But it is so easy for a student to fall through the cracks, linger on the fringes, keep quiet, and not be noticed much—especially at middle- and high-school levels where students are with each teacher just a part of the day. Here's a tool to keep that from happening. It's a way to deliberately focus on what you know about each student.

The teacher-student relationship, like any other relationship in the school community, is continually in play. This means that hundreds of small, everyday interactions are opportunities to seize (or miss) building the kinds of trusting relationships that impact student outcomes in desired ways. So, let's not miss even one such opportunity! Let's show students that our relationships with them matter to us.

Steps:

1. Review Worksheet **R.15a, Signs of Quality Teacher-Student Relationships**. Think about your students and whether they show these signs. Think about yourself and your behaviors and the signals that your behaviors give about your teacher-student relationships.

2. Discuss this worksheet with colleagues. Add ideas to the list.

3. The signs of good relationships can serve as a backdrop to the relationship inspection activity that follows. Keep Worksheet R.15a handy as a reference.

4. Read through the steps for a relationship inspection for each of your classes. Find these on **Worksheet R.15b, Guide for Relationship Inspection**. This process helps you examine and reflect on what you know about each student. It will inspire you to dig into realizing what you have observed, heard, wondered, or assumed about the student.

5. Find quiet time to follow the guide, thoughtfully considering each student. On **Worksheet R.15c, Relationship Inspection Record**, write something you know about students, attend to where you are uncertain or struggle to answer, and note patterns in what you know about kids.

6. Follow steps 7 through 10 on the guide to continue learning and making observations about what you learn.

Other good uses of relationship inspections:

Be aware of good-relationship signs that stretch beyond the teacher-student connections. In all **encounters among anyone in the school community**, we want to see that

- Collaboration, kindness (not criticism), inclusion (not discrimination) are the norms.
- Everyone can count on being respected.
- Appreciation and acceptance of individual and cultural differences are the norms.
- Members are truthful and trustworthy.
- Everyone can feel safe—physically and emotionally.
- Students and adults advocate for themselves and each other.
- Everyone's voice is invited and valued; all members can feel that they belong.
- Students can count on adults (and adults can count on each other) to have their backs.
- Everyone can feel free from exclusion, derision, stereotyping, or bullying.
- Everyone keeps learning and growing.
- Expressions of gratitude are ubiquitous.
- Everyone matters and knows it.

Don't limit relationship inspection to students. This is a critical strategy for your students. But every staff member, too, deserves to be known. Try the same tactic for the adults in the school. Get a list. Write down something you know about each one. When names draw blanks—make a plan to learn about those people. Try the same inspection with students' parents.

Leaders, this is a must for you! How well do you know your staff members? Follow this same practice to check up on your relationships with your colleagues. Then, if you're brave, start examining what you know about students or families!

Signs of Quality
Teacher-Student Relationships

As you consider the extent and health of your relationships with students, keep these signs in mind. Watch for them. Cultivate them.

The students:

- Appear to be comfortable with the teacher
- Believe that the teacher likes them
- Feel noticed (they don't look alienated)
- Feel safe (they don't look scared or wary)
- Each have a voice and use it comfortably; are free to ask questions
- Show signs of engagement with the teacher and the class
- Exhibit high motivation to perform well academically
- Say they feel respected by the teacher
- Show respect to other students
- Laugh, smile, show signs of enjoyment

The teacher:

- Is warm, agreeable, patient, and empathetic to all students
- Shows that she/he likes the students, wants to be with them, wants to teach them
- Encourages autonomy for students (in contrast to control and contingent regard)
- Is positive and affirming in explicit and implicit messages and in body language
- Shows an understanding of the needs, characteristics, and interests of the age group
- Puts serious effort (visibly) into getting to know students as individuals
- Shows genuine interest in students' overall (not just academic) wellbeing
- Accepts and respects every student's culture and individuality
- Believes that each student can succeed and shows it
- Notices, appreciates, and affirms everybody's talents
- Helps students meet their academic and social goals; affirms all accomplishments
- Asks for and listens to all students' opinions, ideas, and perspectives
- Sets high expectations for each student and helps students reach them
- Invites student participation in decisions that affect them
- Does what she/he says; follows through
- Makes contact with every student every day
- Is honest, authentic (not phony), and direct—no game-playing or mixed messages
- Does not threaten, yell, shame, label, judge, or belittle students
- Shows absolutely no favoritism, bias, or predetermined judgments
- Enjoys humor and uses it appropriately; laughs and smiles a lot

Guide for Relationship Inspection

Use this guide to inspect the teacher-student relationship you have with each of your students. Use Worksheet R.15c, Relationship Inspection, or another way to record the students' names and your actions as described below.

1. Get a list of your students. If you have several classes, get a list for each class.

2. Next to each name, write down something you know about that student. This needs to be something other than their grades or work performance or classroom behavior. It must be something personal—the kinds of friends they have, some outside interest or activity, something about their families, or some other non-academic information. (You may need to make several copies of Worksheet R.15c.)

3. Ask yourself: *How easy was this to do for each student?*

4. Ask yourself: *Do I know as much about each student as a person as I should, or as I could? Or as I thought I did?*

5. Mark the names of students for whom you couldn't think of anything—or names on which you hesitated or had to think a long time.

6. Ask yourself: *Is there any pattern that stands out as to which students I know better?* (i.e., Are they the vocal students? The troublesome ones? Those whose parents I know?)

7. Keep these lists handy. Look at them often. Note the students with names marked.

8. Make it a point to learn something about each student.

9. Add to these lists. Keep learning about your students.

10. Once in a while, start fresh on the list. Compare to the earlier list to see what you've learned and how your relationships with students have changed.

Name _____

Relationship Inspection Record

Using the guide provided on Worksheet R.15b, examine your connection with each student and make notes about what you learn from the process.

X	Student Name	Something I Know	Date

Patterns I notice:

Tool 16 SPARKING CLASS CONNECTIONS

✳ **Purpose:** Build class unity to expand a sense of group identity and connection

👤 **User(s):** Leaders, Teachers, students

📚 **Leader Resource:**

Building Brilliant Schools by Dr. Andy Parker, (2021), Chapters 5 through 7

📝 **Supplies:**

Worksheet R.16a, Pass-Around Class Poem

Worksheet R.16b, Strike Up the Class Spirit!

Supplies needed for any class-unity projects students decide to pursue

Description:

Any traditions, symbols, or group creations or projects promote class spirit, unity, and feelings of belonging for all members. Make a habit of including activities that deepen a sense of togetherness— of "our class"— for students. This tool gives two strategies for getting started plus a few other suggestions. But the feeling of being part of the group really blossoms when the class members hatch the ideas and processes together. So, envision yourself as the spark that gets class unity underway

Steps:

1. **Develop a class handshake (could be a no-touch "handshake")**. Class members can work in pairs or small groups to come up with ideas and make proposals to the class. At some point, you'll probably need to take a vote—unless a general consensus is able to be reached. If you find yourself in a climate of a health crisis, such as a pandemic—the handshake might need to become no-touch hand signals in the air that can be done at a distance. Once agreed upon, use the gesture for greeting, parting, and other times of connection. In general, when a private handshake is adopted, the group members agree to keep it secret from outsiders.

2. **Create a class poem together**.
   • Ask students to think about their hopes for the class or for the school or the school year or for themselves during the school year. This might be something that will happen, or won't happen, or that the class will accomplish, or try, or do together. Encourage a wide range of ideas. Give the class 5 to 7 minutes to think and jot down their individual ideas, privately.

- Tell students to select the most important, unique, or interesting hope from their personal brainstormed collection. Tell them they'll be putting this into a one-sentence statement. (They state the hope clearly, but briefly). Let them know they will write this, using one sentence, right into a group poem. Tell them that the poem probably won't rhyme and does not have to. (Yes, some kids might get creative and write a short, rhyming couplet of two lines!)

- Use **Worksheet R.16a, Pass-Around Class Poem**, to collect their hopes and form a poem. You may need to staple together two copies of the worksheet to make room for all lines.

- Each student completes the phrase that begins *I hope . . .* (**Note:** The class poem can begin any number of other ways: *I wish . . . I believe . . .* , **or** *In this class, we are committed to . . . etc.*) They then fold the paper back along the bottom of the line so that the other writers will not see their hope, and pass it along to the next person. If needed, the teacher can help with the folding between writers. Be sure you, the teacher, add your line to the poem too.

- The class will enjoy sharing their group composition. You may want to enlist a couple of students to re-write the completed "epic" onto a large poster.

3. **Other ideas: There are dozens of other ways to "grow" cohesion and belongingness in a class.** Challenge students to think about symbols, projects, traditions, declarations, joint projects, or outreaches that will build class spirit and sense of "We're in this together!"

  - Distribute **Worksheet R.16b, Strike Up the Class Spirit**, to pairs or small groups of students. Use a collaborative group process for students to brainstorm other good ideas for class unity. (This can be such things as a community service project, a class logo, song, flag, mascot, constitution, list of class values or class commitments, etc. Keep some ideas up your sleeve, but let them come up with their own. If you add to the idea pool, make your suggestions no more numerous or important than any other member of the group!)

  - Each group can share its best idea and the whole class can vote on one. Or the class might decide on more than one and send different groups off to get started on each.

Pass-Around Class Poem

Finish the sentence with a line that expresses your hope.

I hope _____

I hope _____

I hope _____

I hope _____

I hope _____

I hope _____

I hope _____

I hope _____

I hope _____

I hope _____

I hope _____

I hope _____

I hope _____

Name _____

Strike Up the Class Spirit!

Work together in your group to identify four good ideas of symbols, traditions, or actions that will involve the entire class to show something about who you are as a class. Think about helping everyone feel a greater sense of belonging and connection to each other. On one of the drums, describe, diagram, or sketch each idea. Give it a label.

Now, choose your best idea. Write more details about what the class would do and how the tradition or action would work.

Tool 17   RELATIONSHIP SELFIES

✳ Purpose: Identify qualities of good peer relationships; strengthen peer relationships

⚇ User(s): Leaders, teachers, students

📚 Leader Resource:

Building Brilliant Schools by Dr. Andy Parker, (2021), Chapters 5 through 7

📝 Supplies:

Worksheet R.17, Demonstrate, Click, & Share

Cell phones or other devices with cameras

Selfie stick (optional)

Drawing supplies (for alternatives to camera shot)

Description:

How can you tell when relationships in the classroom are good quality? What kinds of behaviors or attributes show connections or contacts among students that lead to students feeling safe, valued, equal, included, and respected? How do these behaviors look?

This active tool gets students (of any age) focused on just what it is that makes healthy contacts and relationships among peers at school. Students collaborate to answer such questions as those in the paragraph above and in Step 1 below. Then they put their answers into action by demonstrating, using a favorite activity—snapping pictures of themselves.

Steps:

1. Give students a few questions (orally, or in writing) to get them thinking about relationships in the classroom. You can use such questions as

   What kind of relationships do you want to experience in the classroom (or school)?

   How would you name or label or describe relationships that make you feel welcome, comfortable, safe, or valued?

   How can you tell if such relationships exist?

   What do such relationships look like?

   What are some of the actions or behaviors that show these relationships?

2. Suggest that students start picturing in their minds some scenarios, situations, contacts, or behaviors that demonstrate actions that help build and spread quality relationships or connections.

3. Tell students that they will join in pairs (or groups of three or four—whatever you think will work best). In their groups, they will collaborate to brainstorm visible characteristics of quality relationships or interactions in the classroom or school.

4. Move to groups. Give each group a copy of **Worksheet R.17, Demonstrate, Click, & Share**. Review the instructions on the worksheet together.

5. Allow 15 minutes or so for students to complete Step 1 on the worksheet.

6. Move the groups along to Step 2 on the worksheet, where they plan for selfies.

7. Provide time for them to take selfies and re-take until they get the right picture. Of course, you'll need to monitor the appropriateness of their pictures.

8. Next, tell them to be ready to share and explain their selfies. Each group could write a label and a caption for each selfie.

Note: If actually taking selfies is not possible, students can draw what the selfie would look like for each scenario—using stick figures, if needed.

9. Find a way to print these so they have copies in hand—or a way for these to be projected onscreen! If they can be printed, you can create a selfie wall, poster, or mural—with the labels and captions attached for each example. Be sure to create some way and space for these to be shared. Students might have good ideas about how to do this! Add your selfie to the mix.

10. As a follow-up, students (and you) can be watchful for situations in which they actually catch each other **doing** the good-relationship behaviors recommended by their selfies. You or they could capture these moments on camera!

Note: You may find that students think of including the teacher or teachers or other adults in the school in some of the selfies. After all, relationships in the classroom extend beyond the peers—particularly if you widen the assignment to the school beyond the classroom (unless you limit the assignment specifically to peer relationships).

Name _____

Demonstrate, Click, & Share

Step 1. With your group, brainstorm actions or behaviors that show what good peer relationships look like. Think about the contacts you would like to have with others. You can write words or phrases, but be sure to think about actions and ideas that can be demonstrated in some way. Remember, you'll be showing these in selfies!

_____

_____

_____

_____

_____

_____

_____

Step 2. Now go back and choose your top two. Describe or draw what you will catch on camera. Describe or draw in detail what you will show.

Step 3. When you all agree, set up for the selfie . . . and CLICK!

Tool 18

PERSPECTIVE-TAKING

✳ **Purpose:** Practice considering the perspectives of another person to improve peer relationships and other relationships in the school community

👤 **User(s):** Leaders, teachers, students

📚 **Leader Resource:**

Building Brilliant Schools by Dr. Andy Parker (2021), Chapters 5 through 7

📝 **Supplies:**

Worksheet R.18, Perspective-Taking Trades

Description:

Perspective-taking is actively looking beyond your own point of view and considering how someone else might perceive or experience a situation. To take the perspective of another, you'll need to try to notice and understand the feelings, thoughts, and motivations of the other person. You'll need to learn some things about the other person in order to make assumptions about how they see things. In addition, it requires you to identify your own intentions, feelings, thoughts, and motivations about a situation so that you can notice how they help or hinder your abilities to learn about the other person. All these are critical relationship skills for all members of the school community. And they are skills that can be taught.

This tool offers a strategy to begin the practice of perspective-taking. **Apply it to**

• **Students** taking one another's perspectives

• **Staff members** taking one another's perspectives

• **Leaders taking** one or more staff members' perspectives

• **Staff members or students** taking a leader's perspectives

• Leaders and other staff members taking **parents' perspectives**

Keep in mind that the "students" may also be adults. Whatever the teaching situation, the leader or teacher should practice the steps (below) first with other adults. Research finds that when students of any age gain perspective-taking skills, they are far more able to be kind and considerate, to work well with others, to tune into the needs and feelings of others, and to become comfortable members of social groups.

Steps:

1. Take a closer look at what is involved in perspective-taking.
   Most perspective-taking practices advise these four phases:

   a) Temporarily (and intentionally) setting aside your own thoughts, feelings, intentions, and motivations

   b) Looking for clues to help you consider the thoughts, feelings, intentions, and motivations of the other person (or persons)

   c) Deciding if your behavior or attitude needs to change—based on what you've found out about the other person (in step b)

   d) Taking action to make changes

2. Leaders or teachers: Be the model. Students (or colleagues) learn these skills by watching you. In real-time, real-life situations where students are watching, take some moments to suspend your own perspective and look at the circumstance from another person's point of view. Get in the habit of watching others for clues as to how they might view a situation. Tune into subtle actions, reactions, expressions, attitudes, body language that give you information. Adapt your behavior to your guesses about what the other person's perspective might be.

   Show, by your actions, that you are seeking to understand another's prospective. Tell them what you hear them saying. Describe the clues you pick up and what they lead you to think about what the other person thinks, feels, desires, or intends. Ask the other person to let you know if what you think you understand is on the right track.

3. Share with students a description of what perspective-taking is and why it is important. Use the information from Step 1 above and from the description on the previous page. Take some times for discussions about the components of perspective-taking:

   Thoughts—Discuss the reality that different people understand or think about one situation differently. Use some hypothetical situations for students to identify different thoughts the people involved might have.

   Feelings—Make sure students understand that all the feelings that arise in them or others in a situation are valid. Discuss some of the kinds of feelings (positive and prickly) that might arise when there is a situation encompassing differences of viewpoints. Use some hypothetical situations for students to identify feelings.

Motivations—Define motivations (the reasons or forces behind someone's actions). Use some hypothetical situations for students to discuss possible motivations behind someone's behavior (or different persons' behaviors) in the situation.

Intentions—Define intentions (the purpose, goal, or desire someone has in mind in a situation). Use some hypothetical situations for students to discuss possible intentions involved in someone's viewpoint or behavior in the scenario. (Did the person intend to hurt someone else? Did they intend to disrupt the class? Did they intend to hang on to some of their personal power or self-esteem? Did they intend to protect themselves?)

4. Emphasize the idea that it is okay and normal for people to have different opinions. Discuss the difference between agreeing with someone and hearing/acknowledging their point of view.

5. Working with the whole group, use hypothetical or common situations to look at all the perspectives involved in the situation. Emphasize the importance of connecting people's actions with their perspectives (including the four elements in Step 3 above). Discuss how the actions of each person involved in your scenario affected the other persons. Use these situations to practice looking for clues to understand the actions of each person involved.

6. Then actively practice perspective-taking. Start with a hypothetical situation. Provide students with a video, or an oral or written description of a contact, conflict, disagreement, or difference of viewpoint interaction between two people. Split the student group into pairs. Each student will take on the character of one of the persons as they role-play the situation.

7. After hearing the scenario description and participating in role-play to recreate it, students follow the instructions on **Worksheet R.18, Perspective-Taking Trades,** to summarize what they understand to be the other person's perspective and respond to other's assumptions about their own perspectives.

8. Students **trade worksheets** to see what each one wrote. The receiver uses the second column to respond to the guesses made about his or her perspective.

9. Students trade back and complete Steps 6 and 7 on the sheet.

10. Repeat this process with real situations that arise in the classroom so students can practice taking perspectives of real (rather than hypothetical) persons.

11. Include time for students to discuss the perspectives and responses, what they learned, and what they decided to do differently.

Name _____

Perspective-Taking Trades

Follow the steps to practice taking someone else's perspective.

1. **Briefly tell what happened:**

2. **Make some guesses about the other person's perspective.**

I guess they were thinking

I guess they were feeling

I guess that the motivations (reasons behind the actions) were

I guess that their intentions (what they meant to do) were

4. **Give your response to the other person's guesses.**

Circle what they got right.

What did they not understand?

What impressions of theirs do you want to correct?

3. Trade Papers

5. Trade Papers

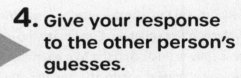

6. **Read the response to your guesses. What did you learn?**

7. **What actions of yours should change?**

50 Tools for Building Brilliant Schools, copyright © 2022 by Dr. Andy Parker

Tool 19 — FAMILY CONNECTIONS

✳ **Purpose:** Improve communication between the school and students' homes; build trusting relationships with students' parents

👤 **User(s):** Leaders, teachers, parents

📚 **Leader Resource:**

Building Brilliant Schools by Dr. Andy Parker (2021), Chapters 5 through 7

📝 **Supplies:**

Worksheet R.19, The Language of Connection

Description:

Meaningful communication with home matters. Brilliant schools understand that communication with parents and guardians is an important tool when it comes to forging a home-school relationship. Research shows that parental engagement with the school has a stronger positive impact on student success than even factors like socioeconomic status. Good connections between teachers and parents lead to significant increases in homework assignment completion, with the greatest gains for at-risk students. They contribute to greater engagement for students in their classrooms and higher participation for parents in students' learning. Students feel stable when there is a comfortable information flow between school and home (Lim, 2018, pp.1–2).

As important as we know good school-home communication is, we still face barriers to home-school connections. And many of those barriers are frustrating. Even though technology has enabled us to make contacts readily with most families, real barriers remain. This tool gives educators some tips to create safer, more humane and welcoming, and more productive communication with families by examining the language we use to communicate. In following any suggestions below, be sure that translations to a parent's language are available.

Steps:

1. First of all, keep in mind that one of the barriers to good home-school connection is present and past relationships between schools and parents. All those parents were once students. And sometimes schools have not been welcoming or nurturing to parents. You can't know what experiences they carry with them from the past (even their past as the students themselves) into their child's school experience.

2. Then, early in the year, work with teachers and other leaders to create a VERY quick questionnaire about home-to-school communication. Ask families to identify the best way (for them) to give and receive communication (i.e., call, text, email, "snail" mail, something else they suggest, or even home visits for certain circumstances). Follow their preferred method.

3. As a leader or teacher, begin the first week of school with positive communication to the home. I'll say that again: **positive communication**. Don't let that first touch with a family be negative. That's lousy—for all involved. Plus, it doesn't serve to support your relationship with your student. This communication can come from any of the student's teachers or the school leader. Collaborate with the adults who work with each child to find a positive message that can be sent to the family—to tell about something noticed, an accomplishment, a great personality trait, an observed helpful behavior for others, a good attitude, a skill used, etc.

4. Keep up this practice throughout the school year. Parents of each student should get several positive messages through the weeks and months. These boost relationships all around, help kids and families feel a sense of belonging, and help parents feel hopeful for their students' well-being at school. When problems arise, the school has set a basis for a trusting relationship with parents. Parents will be more open to hearing about concerns and to joining the school personnel in finding solutions and support for their children.

5. Take care with how you deliver messages. Work to give many more positive than negative impressions, and always include positive when your contact involves a concern. The language of connection takes some forethought and insight. Find a way to think ahead and gather questions or statements or statement stems that will promote caring, respectful relationships.

6. **Worksheet R.19, The Language of Connection**, provides a way for leaders and teachers to work together, in pairs, teams, or other small groups to prepare for conversations with parents. Use the examples provided to trigger your thinking. Add other examples in both columns to practice asking questions and delivering comments in positive ways.

7. Add to this collection over time. Support one another as colleagues with new ideas for broadening your language of connection with parents. Tell each other which ideas worked. Listen to parent feedback related to your communication. Ask them such questions as: *How am I doing at keeping you informed? Has this conversation been helpful? Have you been able to tell me your opinions and ideas?*

Name _____

The Language of Connection

1. In the left column, note some questions or statements that might be part of a conversation with a student's parent when you call or text to address a concern.

2. In the right column, note a replacement question or statement. Remember that not every contact should be motivated by a problem or concern. So, gather communication ideas for both concerns and informative or congratulatory situations.

Instead of this:	Start with that:
I am calling to let you know of a problem I am having with . . . _____	*Good morning/afternoon. This is a good news phone call/text. I can't wait to tell you about...*
_____ has been better, but . . .	*I can tell that _____ is working on what we talked about. Thank you for talking with him/her.*
(Student name) did _____. Will you address it?	*Can you help me with_____?*
_____keeps happening. Will you talk to _____ about _____? I find that (Student name) isn't listening.	*You are the expert when it comes to _____ I'm hoping you can help me understand about _____*
This is the _____ time I am calling you.	*I'd love to tell you about . . .* *Is there a better time to reach you?*

Tool 20

REFLECTING ON THE TOOLS

Purpose: Examine personal experience working with the tools in this Relationship Pillar

User(s): Leaders, teachers, (students, optional)

Leader Resource:

Building Brilliant Schools by Dr. Andy Parker, (2021), Chapters 5 through 7

Supplies:

Worksheet R.20, Looking Back and Looking Forward
A list of the tools that have been used from this chapter
Results of completed tasks from tools in this chapter

Description:

This tool offers a way for those who have used the tools in this section to reflect on what they have done and learned. In addition, it inspires a look forward as to what concepts, behaviors, or goals they will develop and use in the future.

Steps:

1. Distribute copies of **Worksheet R.20, Looking Back and Looking Forward**, as a guide. Also provide a list of the tools that have been used by individuals or groups in their work together. In addition, if the folks reflecting have saved any products or worksheets from the individual tools—these would be helpful to have on hand as participants reflect over their experiences.

2. With the worksheet as a guide, individuals reflect on their own and note their reflections. If students have used some of the tools, you might invite them to do the same or similar process of reflection.

3. Depending on the setting, groups may choose to share and discuss their reflections. Teams or grade-level groups or entire faculties may wish to use the reflections to set goals together.

Name _____

Looking Back and Looking Forward

Reflect on what you learned, thought, experienced, and wish to do further with the tools in this pillar. Write a comment in each category.

Most powerful tool for me, and why	
Most challenging tool for me, and why	
A key idea I learned	
Tool that I think will be great for my students, and why	
Tool that's been most helpful to my group of colleagues, and why	
Something I learned about myself while using these tools	
Two goals I want to set for myself related to the tools in this pillar	

Chapter 3

Tools for Your **EXPECTATIONS** Toolbox

Nobody rises to low expectations.

– Steve Maraboli, Behavioral Scientist, Author

This collection of tools focuses on research-based traits, beliefs, and practices that are identified as key influences on the development of the equitable, high expectations that we want to develop and show for all students (and others) in our school communities.

⚙ Definitions

Expectations:
> *beliefs about and in persons, about the potential they have to achieve, and about their probable behaviors or characteristics now or in the future*

Bias:
> *a tendency to believe that some people, ideas, etc. are better than others, which often results in treating some people unfairly (Facing History, 2021, para. 5); a natural inclination for or against an idea, object, group, or individual. It is often learned and is highly dependent on variables like a person's socioeconomic status, race, ethnicity, education, background, etc. (Bias, 2021, para.1)*

Implicit (Unintentional) Bias:
> *a judgment or behavior that results from subtle cognitive processes—attitudes or stereotypes—that often operate at a level below conscious awareness and without intentional control (Facing History, 2021, para. 7).*

⚙ Key Benefits of High Teacher Expectations for Students

• When teachers expect that certain students **will** show greater intellectual or academic growth, the students **do** show greater intellectual or academic growth.

• When teachers expect students to go on to graduate from college, they are more likely to do so.

• Teacher belief in a student's academic capabilities improves students' attitudes towards school and influences students to believe they will do well in school.

• Teacher belief in a student's academic capabilities positively affects students' attitudes towards school.

- Students respond to high expectations by internalizing them, thus boosting their own academic expectations.

- Teachers who overestimate the ability of students get better academic results (than teachers who underestimate the ability).

- Teachers' high expectations set the tone for expectations students have of other students. And when peers have high expectations of one another, they all tend to do better.

- Teacher expectations are more predictive of future educational attainment than such other factors as academic effort, motivations, race, high school courses taken, parents' educational level, and parents' expectations for their children.

- Effects of teacher expectations accumulate over time; and the influence grows significantly stronger as students progress through school.

⚙ Consequences of Low Teacher Expectations for Students

- Communicating low expectations has more power to limit student achievement than communicating high expectations has to raise student performance.

- When the teacher does not believe that students can perform at high levels, the students don't.

- When a student senses that a teacher has low expectations, the student has low expectations for herself or himself. This decreases student performance and negatively affects self-belief and feelings about school.

- Teacher doubts confirm students' worst fears about their potential.

- Teachers who underestimate the ability of students get lower academic results than teachers who overestimate students' abilities.

- A teacher's low expectations of a student set the tone for expectations other students will have of that individual.

- Negatively-biased teacher expectations have a detrimental influence—not only on a student's current and future academic performance, but also on the student's future career.

⚙ Expectations Interventions

It is possible to raise teacher expectations to prevent low or underestimated expectations from having detrimental effects on student achievement—and also, to promote the many benefits of high teacher expectations! Research has found that when teachers are committed to the following processes, their work is effective in raising teacher expectations and, subsequently, student achievement:

1. Understanding that effects of teacher expectations have to do with attributes, attitudes, beliefs, and stereotypes held by the teachers rather than with the actual academic characteristics or potential of the students

2. Raising awareness of one's expectations

3. Investigating and addressing the beliefs, attitudes, and biases underlying the expectations

4. Changing teacher expectations around communicating expectations

Note: For a more complete discussion of expectations definitions, benefits, consequences, and interventions, as well as a more thorough exploration of bias and the sources of our bias, see Chapters 8 through 10 in **Building Brilliant Schools: What G.R.E.A.T. Leaders Do Differently**, by Dr. Andy Parker (2021).

Use the next page to keep notes from your reading of those chapters.

⚙ Expectations Tools for Brilliant Schools

Each of the following tools teaches or strengthens one or more of the skills known to nurture equal, high, and fair expectations.

21. Expectations Inspection (Expectations Awareness)

22. Inviting Insights (Expectations Awareness)

23. Dialogue Memos (Expectations Awareness and Intervention)

24. Discipline Scrutiny (Expectations Awareness and Bias Awareness)

25. On the Line (Bias Awareness)

26. Bias Alert! (Bias Awareness)

27. Project Bias Reduction (Bias Awareness and Reduction)

28. High-Expectations Behaviors (Expectations Intervention)

29. Expectations by the Bucketful (Expectations Intervention)

30. Reflecting on the Tools (Self-Evaluation on Use of Expectations Tools)

Notes from Expectations Chapters

Building Brilliant Schools: What G.R.E.A.T. Leaders Do Differently, Chapters 8–10

As you read about Expectations, jot down key ideas or points that you want to remember from each chapter.

Chapter 8, What Are Expectations?

Expectations

Bias

Implicit Bias

Chapter 9, Why Expectations?

Chapter 10, How Do G.R.E.A.T. Leaders Get Results with Expectations?

Tool 21

EXPECTATIONS INSPECTION

⊛ **Purpose:** Increase awareness of and examine expectations teachers have for students
Increase awareness of and examine expectations leaders have for staff members

☺ **User(s):** Leaders, teachers, students

📚 **Leader Resource:**

Building Brilliant Schools by Dr. Andy Parker (2021), Chapters 8 through 10

📝 **Supplies:**

Worksheet E.21, Investigating My Expectations

Description:

With this tool, leaders or teachers dig into the task of putting their expectations (of their staff members or students) under a microscope. You might assume you know your attitudes and beliefs about each staff member or student. But when have you intentionally checked those assumptions? This "Expectations Inspection" guides you through a process for doing just that. The process will take some time, but what you learn will be extremely valuable (and perhaps surprising).

Steps:

1. Leaders, get a roster of your staff members or particular group of staff members. Teachers, get out a roster of your students (or a roster for each class). Use **Worksheet E.21, Investigating My Expectations**, to guide this process. Transfer each roster to a copy of this sheet. Then use it (or a template you create yourself) to collect your observations.

2. Next to each name, write down an impression or assumption you have of the student or staff member. Use a word or phrase that encapsulates your assessment or level of expectation for the student (examples: *promising, reluctant, lagging, engaged, disruptive, eager, high-performing, struggler; responsible; hard worker, great talent; minimal effort; over her head in this class/job*).

3. Leaders, rate each staff member on the level of how you expect them to fare in doing their job well. Teachers, rate each student on the level of how you expect them to fare academically in your class. You can use **Scale A** shown on the worksheet (or another scale you devise) to show what you think the individual's skills and abilities are to handle the work (on the job or in the class).

4. Rate each staff member or student on what you assume about how hard they will work in this job or class. Use **Scale B** shown on the worksheet (or other scale you devise).

5. After you've done this, look at your list and ratings. Then take the important step of analyzing your results.

Leaders, think about staff members' characteristics; watch for patterns:

- What do you notice about members for whom you have **lower** expectations? Note any patterns in characteristics (ethnicity, gender, personal traits, experience level, perceived emotional maturity, previous job performance, family structure or obligations, age, socioeconomic status, where they live, friends, etc.)
- What do you notice about members for whom you have **higher** expectations? Note any patterns in characteristics (same traits as above).
- Specifically look at different categories of people, and check to see if there are patterns in your beliefs or expectations that pertain to whole groups.

Teachers, think about students' characteristics; watch for patterns:

- What do you notice about students for whom you have **lower** expectations? Note any patterns in characteristics (ethnicity, gender, personal traits, physical maturity, friends, perceived emotional maturity, parents who are involved in the school (or not), socioeconomic status, previous academic performance, etc.)
- What do you notice about students for whom you have **higher** expectations? Note any patterns in characteristics (same traits as above).
- Specifically look at different categories of students, and check to see if there are patterns in your beliefs or expectations about any categories.

6. Take some time to step back, consider thoughtfully what you've done and discovered, and ask yourself this: *From reviewing this list (or multiple rosters), what can I learn about my expectations? What might this mean about my beliefs? What is most striking?*

7. This can be tough work. It requires self-awareness and honesty. If you work with a team of teachers, you might do this individually and then join with others to collaborate on your ratings. Think of this activity as a starting point. It can begin to give you clues about your expectations. Come back and use this tool again in several weeks—after you have used some of the other tools to work at consistently high expectations for all students. Compare your results.

Name _____

Investigating My Expectations

Follow Steps 1–4 in the instructions to examine and record something about your expectations for each of the students in this class (or each staff member). Then complete Steps 5–7 for this tool. Keep notes in a separate log.

Class/Group _____ **Date** _____

Name	Impression/Assumption About This Individual	Rating: Expectations for Performance	Rating: Prediction for Effort Level

Scale A for Expected Achievement or Performance Level:

1 *Very Low;* 2 *Low;* 3 *Average;* 4 *Above Average;* 5 *Strong;* 6 *Excellent*

Scale B for Expected Effort Level:

1 *Disengaged;* 2 *Minimal;* 3 *Intermittent;* 4 *Mostly consistent;* 5 *Optimum*

Tool 22

INVITING INSIGHTS

✳ **Purpose:** Solicit observations of others to increase awareness of your own expectations

👤 **User(s):** Leaders, teachers, students

📚 **Leader Resource:**

Building Brilliant Schools by Dr. Andy Parker, (2021), Chapters 8 through 10

📝 **Supplies:**

Worksheet E.22a, Expectations Insights (From Staff Member to Leader)

Worksheet E.22b, Expectations Insights (From Colleague to Colleague)

Worksheet E.22c, Expectations Insights (From Student to Teacher)

Description:

Often, others can give you information about your attitudes, beliefs, and expectations that you might not notice in yourself. That's because they have the benefit of observing your behaviors and listening to what you say and how you say it. This tool offers some strategies with which you can ask trusted colleagues and your students to give feedback about your expectations. This applies to leaders' expectations of their staff members or teachers' expectations of their students.

Steps for Leaders Requesting Impressions from Staff Members:

1. If you're brave enough, ask your staff members to give their feedback about what they perceive to be your expectations about their job abilities and performance. Ask them to watch for signs and messages that you give about what you expect of them. Ask them to be on the alert for differences in the way you relate to different staff members—things like your responses to them, demeanor around them, asking their opinions, inviting them to participate, initiating contact with them, sharing leadership, giving feedback, etc.

2. Ask staff members to complete **Worksheet E.22a, Expectations Insights (From Staff Member to Leader)**. Or, they can give you notes or verbal feedback, if they wish. Give them the option to remain anonymous.

3. Follow up! Embrace the impressions eagerly and seriously. Find ways to ask for more suggestions. Make plans to act on what you learn. Demonstrate that you are listening and that you will work to state clearly and hold consistently to fair, equitable expectations for your staff. Let them see, as well, that you're dedicated to helping them meet expectations.

Steps for Requesting Impressions from Colleagues:

1. If you're brave enough, ask a trusted colleague to observe you in the classroom. This may be most do-able for team members!) Ask them to watch for signs and messages that you give about what you expect of students or staff members. Ask them to be on the alert for differences in the way you relate to students—things like responses, asking questions, inviting them to participate, initiating contact with them, or giving directions, help, criticism, discipline, etc. Listen carefully to the feedback your colleagues give.

2. Ask the colleague to complete **Worksheet E.22b, Expectations Insights (From Colleague to Colleague)**. Or, they can give you notes or verbal feedback, if they wish. Give them the option to remain anonymous.

3. Follow up! Embrace the impressions eagerly and seriously. Do some tallies of responses. Look for patterns in the feedback. Ask for clarification. Ask for suggestions. Make plans to act on what you learn. Let your colleagues see that you are listening and that you will work to state clearly and hold consistently to fair, equitable expectations for your students.

Steps for Requesting Impressions from Students:

1. If you're a teacher, the people who know your expectations best—or at least those who "pick up on them" best even if they're not clearly stated—are the students. Find an appropriate way to survey students to get their feedback on expectations in your classroom.

2. You can use the following **Worksheet E.22c, Expectations Insights (From Student to Teacher)** as a survey, or create other instruments/processes for them to give feedback. You might ask students to design a survey! Make the survey anonymous unless a student chooses otherwise.

3. Follow up! Embrace the impressions eagerly and seriously. Do some tallies of responses. Look for patterns in the feedback. Make plans to act on what you learn. It takes courage to give such feedback to teachers. Make sure that you honor students' input by visibly demonstrating that you have heard it and are acting on it to hold clear, high, equitable expectations for all of them. Find ways to ask for suggestions. Go back and ask students later, "How am I doing?"

Expectations Insights
(From Staff Member to Leader)

This is a request for your observations about the kinds of expectations I demonstrate for my staff members and the ways I communicate those expectations. Reflect on what you see, hear, or otherwise "pick up" from my attitudes, behaviors, or comments. Circle a response for each statement, 1–7. From what you observe and experience . . .

1. I hold high expectations for all staff members.	**Yes**	**No**	**Somewhat**
2. I believe in all staff members' abilities to do their jobs.	**Yes**	**No**	**Somewhat**
3. I expect more from some staff members and less from others.	**Yes**	**No**	**Somewhat**
4. I treat all staff members with equal regard.	**Yes**	**No**	**Somewhat**
5. I communicate expectations clearly.	**Yes**	**No**	**Somewhat**
6. I offer and give adequate support to all staff members to enable them to meet expectations.	**Yes**	**No**	**Somewhat**
7. I give positive reinforcement and helpful feedback equally to all staff members.	**Yes**	**No**	**Somewhat**

Give brief answers to the questions:

8. How can you tell what I expect from you?

9. What signs do you see that show who I expect will be successful at the job they do?

10. Is there anything else you notice related my expectations for staff members' work and abilities?

Expectations Insights
(From Colleague to Colleague)

This is a request for your observations about the kinds of expectations I demonstrate for my students. Reflect on what you see, hear, or otherwise "pick up" from my attitudes, behaviors, or comments. Circle a response for each statement, 1–7. From what you notice . . .

1. I hold high expectations for everyone in my class(es).   **Yes**   **No**   **Somewhat**

2. I believe all students have the ability to do the work in my class(es).   **Yes**   **No**   **Somewhat**

3. I expect more from some students and less from others.   **Yes**   **No**   **Somewhat**

4. I value all of my students equally.   **Yes**   **No**   **Somewhat**

5. My attitudes and actions communicate to students that I believe they all can succeed.   **Yes**   **No**   **Somewhat**

6. I give positive reinforcement and feedback equally to all students.   **Yes**   **No**   **Somewhat**

7. I work hard to help all students, equally, to meet high expectations.   **Yes**   **No**   **Somewhat**

Give brief answers to the questions:

8. What behaviors show you that I do (or do not) expect the same from all students?

9. In your observation, for which students do I have high expectations? And, for which students do I have lower expectations?

10. Is there anything else you notice related my expectations for students' work and abilities?

Expectations Insights
(From Student to Teacher)

This is a request for your feedback on expectations in this classroom. Read each statement. Reflect on what you see, hear, or otherwise "pick up." Circle a response for each statement, 1–7. Sign your name only if you wish.

1. My teacher has high expectations for everyone in the class.   **Yes   No   Somewhat**

2. I believe my teacher expects me to do well in this class.   **Yes   No   Somewhat**

3. I notice that the teacher expects more from some students and less from others.   **Yes   No   Somewhat**

4. The teacher values all of us equally   **Yes   No   Somewhat**

5. The teacher thinks all the students in this class are smart.   **Yes   No   Somewhat**

6. The teacher gives positive feedback to all students, equally.   **Yes   No   Somewhat**

7. The teacher helps us all, equally, to meet expectations for our school work.   **Yes   No   Somewhat**

Give brief answers to the questions:

8. How can you tell what the teacher expects from you?

9. What signs do you see that show who the teacher thinks will succeed in this class?

10. Is there anything else you notice related to the teacher's expectations about students' work and abilities in the classroom?

50 Tools for Building Brilliant Schools, copyright © 2022 by Dr. Andy Parker

Tool 23
DIALOGUE MEMOS

⊛ **Purpose:** Nurture ongoing dialogue that increases awareness of expectations and decreases bias

👤 **User(s):** Leaders, teachers, students

📚 **Leader Resource:**

Building Brilliant Schools by Dr. Andy Parker (2021), Chapters 8 through 10

📝 **Supplies:**

Worksheet E.23, FYI Memos
Blank Memo notes (or index cards, sticky notes, journals, etc.)

Description:

Surveys are great aids to gain feedback from colleagues or students about expectations. But the complexities and habits around expectations aren't solved with an occasional survey. It takes an ongoing dialogue to listen, learn, and change behaviors that lead to attainable, equal expectations. If you've used Tool 22, Expectations Investigations, you will have learned something about others' perceptions of your expectations. Tool 23 sets a process for continued dialogue about expectations. Students give the teacher weekly thoughts about the teacher's expectations. The teacher responds. This takes thoughtfulness, insight, and transparency on the part of both participants in the dialogue. It heightens the awareness of expectations in the classroom—how they are communicated and perceived. It has the great side effects of deepening relationships and decreasing biased expectations.

Steps:

Note: Leaders and teachers can use this same approach with colleagues.

1. Explain the idea and process in order to let students know what to do:

   • Each week, write a memo giving one (or two, if room) thoughts—current observations, feelings, impressions, or suggestions related in some way to expectations in the classroom.
   • Use **Worksheet E.23, FYI Memos**, as a guide. This gives general ideas and shows a format that can be used for the memo process.
   • *Alternative*: If students regularly write in journals, the memos and dialogue might take place there. Students mark something they want the teacher to read and the teacher responds with a note in the journal or clipped to the page.

2. When students finish memos, they'll place these in a specified place for the teacher to read.

3. Within a few days (not many!), the teacher responds to each memo—right on the memo. The response can include:

   • Some indication of what the teacher heard or learned
   • A response to that information
   • An indication of what the teacher intends to do about what has been learned
   • Perhaps a reference to something the student suggested earlier—with the teacher asking "How am I doing with _____ that you suggested last week?"

Note from Dr. Andy: For years, I used students' journals as a source for such dialogues. The topic was not targeted to expectations, but the process of a regular dialogue was invaluable to me as a teacher. I learned so much about how I operated, communicated, and affected individuals. I had a rule that, if a writer was absent, they would write an entry within two days of returning to class. Along the same lines— the students made a rule for me: when I was absent, I was held to the same standard for my response.

Students soon added another rule for me: I had to write something meaningful, substantive. (This is a good process in which to teach students the meaning of the word substantive!) One time, in my haste to catch up when I had been out at a workshop for a few days, I wrote some brief quips such as, "Okay!" or "Really?" or "How insightful!" The next dialogue from one student, Jamie, was this simple entry: "Memo to Andy: I am not writing any more journal entries if you cannot give me back more than an 'Okay' or a 'Really?'" (Lesson learned, Jamie. Thanks, kiddo!)

FYI Memos

Use this as a guide to help you get started on your memo. The ideas are suggestions. You can certainly add your own variations. Just keep your message focused on **expectations** related to academics or other classroom matters. You can cut out this Memo note or create one on a card or other paper.

In your memo, you can

- Ask a question
- Make a comment
- Give a suggestion
- Tell a personal experience
- Ask for help
- Share an observation
- Give a compliment

Some Ideas for Memo Topics

Memo about only 1 or 2 at a time!

- Whether expectations seem equal for all students
- What needs to be clarified
- How you think the teacher views your abilities
- What can be done to help you meet expectations
- Whether expectations are challenging enough
- How the teacher lets you know if you meet expectations
- Whether the teacher thinks you are smart
- Whether the students think other students are capable
- How to help students set high expectations for themselves
- If stated expectations are different from what is really expected
- If there are expectations that are unspoken
- What you need from the teacher
- What the teacher is doing well
- Whether you see the teacher acting on suggestions and feedback

Tool 24

DISCIPLINE SCRUTINY

※ **Purpose:** Increase expectations awareness and bias awareness

👤 **User(s):** Leaders, teachers

📚 **Leader Resource:**

Building Brilliant Schools by Dr. Andy Parker, (2021), Chapters 8 through 10

📝 **Supplies:**

Worksheet E.24, Discipline Tally
Class (or school) Discipline Logs for two weeks

Description:

One effective way to get a sense of your biases and expectations of students is to examine actions around student discipline. This tool outlines a process for keeping a discipline record and analyzing the information to see what you can learn about your expectations for students or various groups of students. This tool can be used for classroom occurrences, for incidents that involve school-mandated consequences, or both.

In 2015, the Civil Rights Project at UCLA released a report that studied what they called "the discipline gap." Examining data from every public school district in the country (showing suspensions of nearly 3.5 million public school students in one school year), researchers noted that this amounted to 18 million days of instruction lost to children in U.S. public schools in just one year. They emphasized the damage to student performance that results from loss of instructional time, noting studies finding that missing three days of school in a month can lower students' standardized reading test scores a full grade level. Also, higher suspension rates are associated with higher delinquency and dropout rates (Losen & Hodson, et al.).

Furthermore, the examination of the suspension data found wide disparities in the use of suspensions for different subgroups. Historically disadvantaged racial, ethnic, and gender subgroups, as well as students with disabilities, have far higher rates of suspension than White students. The rates are highest (by far) for Black males, Latino males, and Black females—with a large percentage in each of these groups being students with disabilities. These researchers strongly assert that "If we ignore the discipline gap, we will be unable to close the achievement gap" (Losen & Hodson, et al., pg. 4).

Other studies find that students of color, particularly Black students, are suspended and expelled far more frequently than their White classmates **for the same or similar offences** (Losen & Sun, et al., 2017).

Steps:

Discipline Log   Class _____ Date Span _____

Student	Date	Issue/Behavior	Discipline Action

1. Read through the steps below. You can prepare to do this strategy on your own. But if you work on a team, it is valuable to do together. It can also be useful for leaders and other administrators to do together by looking at school-wide discipline data.

2. For a period of two weeks, each time you discipline a student or give a consequence for behavior, note the name, date, the issue, and the discipline action. (See above image.)

3. Using two weeks' discipline log and a copy of **Worksheet E.24, Discipline Tally**, do a tally of the discipline actions.

4. Take a hard look at your tallies. Analyze what you see. Ask yourself such questions as:

   • *What do I notice about the students on the list?*

   • *Are there any categories into which they fall (particular ethnicity, gender, low grades, learning difficulty, learning or physical disability, particular socioeconomic level, families with problems, siblings with discipline actions, extrovert, introvert, highly verbal, athletic, strong physically, academic performance, socially well-accepted, tall, small, etc.)?*

   • *Which categories were disciplined the most?*

   • *Were any students given different consequences for the same offense? If so, who got heavier (or lighter) consequences?*

5. Using information from this tally and these questions, explore what the discipline decisions tell you about your expectations or biases related to individuals or student groups.

6. Make a plan to re-examine your discipline choices (or school policies) to show equality, fairness, and commitment to keeping students in school for good instruction.

Discipline Tally

Put your Discipline Log beside this worksheet. Look at one category at a time. Read and think about each name on the log. If a student fits the category, make a tally mark. Skip any that are not applicable. Add other categories that apply to the class.

Characteristic	Tally
Majority ethnicity	
Minority ethnicity	
Gender, male	
Gender, female	
Gender identity, other	
Disability	
Poor academic history	
Good academic history	
History of behavior issues	
Sibling discipline history	
High SES	
Middle SES	
Low SES	
High social acceptance	
Low social acceptance	
Family distress	
Highly verbal	
Language difficulty	

Characteristic	Tally
Good attendance	
Poor attendance	
Family involved in school	
Family not involved	
Physical talents	
Influential Social Group	
Negative Social Group	
Eager participant	
Non-eager participant	
Outgoing	
Shy	
Hygiene irregularities	

Total the tallies for each category. Go back to the instructions for this tool. Complete Steps 4-6 and answer these two questions to guide your analysis and future actions.

What do you notice about how you respond to certain students and their behaviors?

What does your analysis of these tallies lead you to consider doing differently?

Tool 25

ON THE LINE

✳ **Purpose:** Increase bias awareness and contribute to re-thinking expectations and biases

 User(s): Leaders, teachers, students

 Leader Resource:

> *Building Brilliant Schools* by Dr. Andy Parker (2021), Chapters 8 through 10

📝 **Supplies:**

> Worksheet E.25a, Step on the Line (Use with Adults)
> Worksheet E.25b, Step on the Line (Use with Students)
> Masking tape or painter's tape, preferably wide and bright

Description:

This tool outlines a simple activity where participants identify with situations, characteristics, or experiences that are part of their "story." All individuals, including the leader or teacher, show something about themselves. At the same time, they are nudged to re-examine their expectations, preconceptions, and biases of and about others in the group.

Steps:

1. Using wide, colored (not clear) tape, stick down a long straight line across the room. It needs to be long enough that half of the entire group can stand along each side with 2 to 3 feet of space between them.

2. Explain the process to participants. Tell them:

   - This activity is to be done seriously and in complete silence, except for the statements I will make. No talking, whispering, giggling, laughing, eye-rolling, or gesturing.

   - When it is time to start, half of the group will stand on each side of the line—but not directly across from each other.

   - I will read statements, one at a time. The different statements describe a variety of traits, experiences, or characteristics. Each one begins with the instruction: "Step on the line if you . . . "

   - We'll wait a bit to notice who is where; then I'll ask you to step off the line.

3. Start the activity: Invite everyone to take a spot on one side of the line or the other. Read the statements clearly, one at a time. Choose some ideas from the **Worksheet, Step on the Line (E.25a for adults or E.25b for students).** Or replace them with ideas of your own. Add others, if you wish; include questions about recent events in your community, the world, or your school.

4. Leaders and teachers: Take part in the activity. Step on the line when it applies to you.

5. After you read each statement, give time for participants to decide what they will do, and some more time for everyone to notice who has joined the line. Remember to ask everyone to step off the line before you give the next statement.

6. Gather the group together for reflection or discussion or both. Ask a few questions. You don't need to ask them all; it's an activity you can repeat another time. Participants can jot down answers to the questions privately or share their answers with the group.

Ask such questions as these, or create or add your own:

   - *What surprised you? OR What happened that you did not expect?*

   - *What did you learn about some other individuals?*

   - *What did you learn about yourself or about your expectations of others?*

   - *What kinds of feelings did you have as you stepped on the line (or didn't)?*

   - *Did you feel commonality with others?*

   - *What was the hardest part of this?*

   - *Did you notice diversity of the responses?*

   - *Did you learn something about the values of others?*

   - *How did other people's movement affect you?*

   - *How did it feel when you were on the line with very few others?*

   - *Did some of the actions of others change your assumptions about them?*

   - *What will you remember most about what you just experienced?*

   - *What does this activity have to do with our discussion about expectations?*

   - *Given what you learned or noticed, what expectations will you need to change?*

7. Leaders and teachers: Answer these questions too. This strategy will help you get a good look at your own expectations of your co-workers or your students. It is a good starting point from which to examine how what you saw was or was not what you expected.

Step on the Line

Use these questions as a guide to lead the "On the Line" Activity. Give instructions one at a time, waiting long enough for people to decide what to do and then to notice what others have done. The leader should participate, too. Remind participants that any move they make is voluntary. They should feel no pressure to step on the line.

Step on the line if you . . .

would like to be closer to your family members

feel confident about your work at this school

believe that everyone in this group is competent at their jobs

know anyone who has died young

consider yourself tolerant

have different expectations for different students

are a single parent

have had a broken heart

have been the target of a racist or sexist comment

have been judged or made fun of because of the way you look, dress, or talk

have mastered at least one TikTok dance or challenge

sometimes feel pressured to agree with your leaders or colleagues

have a family member (including yourself) or close friend with a serious illness

have ever taken part in harassing or bullying someone

aren't sure that you are valued by all your colleagues

love to relax by binge-watching TV or videos

have traveled out of the country

have watched a student be teased or excluded and did nothing about it

have ever felt like an outsider in this school community

are worried about the emotional health of a friend or family member

are comfortable asking questions of and giving your opinions to school leaders

like to sing or play a musical instrument

feel that you are a good friend

have felt overwhelmed or anxious in the past week

have ever had a hard time making friends

have felt uncertain about how well you are doing your job

came to school today feeling optimistic

actively support the value and the rights of people who are different from you

Step on the Line

Use these questions as a guide to lead the "On the Line" Activity. Give instructions one at a time, waiting long enough for people to decide what to do and then to notice what others have done. Teachers should participate too. Remind students that any move they make is voluntary. They should feel no pressure to step on the line.

Step on the line if you . . .

rode the bus to school today

feel confident about something you are good at doing

believe that everyone in this class is smart

know anyone who has died young

have had a broken heart

are the oldest child in your family

have been the target of a racist or sexist comment

have been teased or made fun of because of the way you look, dress, or talk

have recently mastered a TikTok dance or challenge

have done something you were pressured to do, but wish you hadn't done it

have felt left out because of your gender

have traveled to another state

sometimes feel embarrassed at school

speak more than one language

have ever done something (on purpose) to make someone else feel uncomfortable

like to watch or take part in sports

have watched someone be bullied but were afraid to speak up

have watched someone be bullied and stepped up to their defense

believe that everyone here has equal value

have ever felt that you did not belong in your class or school

are worried about the emotional or physical health of a friend or family member

had breakfast before you came to school today

like to listen to music

feel that you are a good friend

have felt overwhelmed or anxious in the past week

have ever had a hard time making friends

sometimes feel afraid to come to school

came to school today feeling optimistic

have ever felt misunderstood

Tool 26

BIAS ALERT!

 Purpose: Increase awareness of personal biases

User(s): Leaders, teachers

 Leader Resources:

> *Building Brilliant Schools* by Dr. Andy Parker (2021), Chapters 8 through 10
> The Nordell article:
> https://www.theatlantic.com/science/archive/2017/05/unconscious-bias-training/525405/
> (Short link: https://bit.ly/biasalert)
> *The End of Bias: A Beginning: The Science and Practice of Overcoming Unconscious Bias* (by Jessica Nordell, 2021)

Supplies:

> Worksheet E.26, Flutter Diary
> Information and story from "Description" section below

Description:

This tool outlines a process for super-sensitizing ourselves to implicit bias. It is built around the work of Patricia Devine, a social psychologist from the University of Wisconsin. Her 1989 study on stereotypes and prejudice spurred decades of research on implicit bias (which she also calls *unintentional bias*) and ways to combat it.

Believing that "prejudice is a habit that can be broken," Devine has developed and refined an intervention to combat unintentional bias (Nordell, para. 33)—based on this idea: **If underlying beliefs and prejudices are the cause of biased behavior, then untethering those negative associations could help to eliminate bias**. She believes that 1) People can believe and notice that they might be discriminating. 2) They can identify and own their biases—not ignore or hide them. 3) They can realize that discrimination is a problem; and 4) They can grow in confidence that they can overcome their prejudicial habits. With this foundation of acceptance and belief, they can begin to break the habit.

Jessica Nordell, (2017) is a longtime researcher in the topic of bias. After participating in Devine's training workshop, Nordell says that she began to notice her spontaneous biased reactions to "an almost overwhelming degree." Bias starts, Nordell realized, as "a tiny story, a minor assumption. It is a flicker—unseen, unchecked—that taps at behaviors, reactions, and thoughts" (para. 50–51).

In her article, Nordell recounts a personal tale in which she observed two people (dressed in rumpled, ragged clothing) checking into the upscale hotel where the workshop was held, and spontaneously formed in her mind a story about why they must be there. Assuming that these folks could not possibly be guests at the hotel, she created the explanation that they were probably friends of the clerk, stopping by for a visit. She explains, "It was a tiny story, a minor assumption, but that's how bias starts: as a flicker. And this tiny story flitted through my mind for seconds before I caught it. "My God," I thought, "is this how I've been living?" (para. 50–51).

"Afterward," Nordell says, "I kept watching for that flutter, like a person with a net in hand waiting for a dragonfly. And I caught it, many times. Maybe this is the beginning of how my prejudice ends. Watching for it. Catching it and holding it up to the light. Releasing it. Watching for it again" (2017, para. 50–51).

Steps:

1. Leaders working with a group of other leaders or teachers, or teachers working with each other: Share the text from the "Description" section above. If you want more background on this researcher and the source article from *The Atlantic* (Nordell, 2017), take time to read the entire article first. The web address of this article is shown above (on page 113).

2. I (Dr. Andy) have begun to repeatedly challenge myself, my staff, and all my readers to watch for "that flutter." Take the opportunity to talk about this with your staff and colleagues.

3. Break into pairs or small groups and ask participants to close their eyes and take some time to remember if they have had a similar experience—a time they have felt a flicker of recognition that they are telling themselves a bias-based little story. Perhaps say something like this:

   *Think about this: In your school, how many times have you spoken or thought something judgmental, negative, or demeaning about a parent, colleague, administrator, visitor, or student— something that was triggered in some way by what you assumed—influenced by or related to that person's looks, background, speech, marital status, family, lifestyle, education (how much and from where), level of experience, youth, older age, clothing, hobbies, rumors about relationships or previous jobs, physical condition, ethnicity, gender, gender identity, friends or groups with whom the person associates, religious or spiritual beliefs, etc., etc.? Be honest. This happens all the time! Generally, we educators **do** believe in fairness, equality, and decency. We **do** want to help all the students succeed. It's our passion! It's why we're here. Nevertheless, those implicit biases **do** have some hold on each person—remember: they are unconscious.*

4. Wait a few minutes while people try to "capture" such an experience. Let them know that this does not have to be limited to school situations. It can happen anywhere—on the street, in the grocery store, at your kid's soccer game, at church, etc. Give a few more minutes for participants to jot down a brief description of such an experience. You participate too. **Worksheet E.26, Flutter Diary,** is useful for this practice.

5. Take some time to share and discuss these experiences in the small groups, if you gauge that the participants will be open to doing so. Let participants know that they'll not be expected to show or talk about anything they do not wish to share. One less-threatening approach is to share a scenario that might have been seen by an anonymous observer and what story flitted through that anonymous person's mind.

6. Challenge the group to begin watching for the "flutters" of bias. Suggest to participants that they carry a small notebook around for a few weeks to "catch" and note flutters that will, most certainly, show up more often. They can put a copy of Worksheet E.26 into the notebook to help with analysis of these moments. This will help them examine those small moments and consider what lies behind them. **Unintentional biases are at the base of many of our expectations in our schools.** The more we **catch** the flutters, the more progress we will make in reducing biases and faulty expectations.

7. Gather again to continue addressing this topic. Participants can share what they've learned from their Flutter Diaries. Add other analysis questions as you practice this and share together.

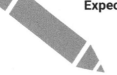

Name (optional) _____

Flutter Diary

Use this diary model to keep track of instances where you get a signal of an unintentional bias. Use questions 1–2 to help you remember and describe the example. Use questions 3–5 to guide your reflection on and analysis of the flutter.

Catch the flutter:

1. What triggered the flutter? (That is, what happened? What did you see or hear?) Describe it briefly.

2. What did you immediately assume? Or, what little story did you tell yourself about the person(s) or about the situation? Write some notes about this.

Dig more deeply:

3. What memories, past experiences, or other influences could be a source or sources of your assumption(s)? Make some notes about this.

4. What might have been faulty about your assumption? Write a phrase or sentence about this.

5. From catching this flutter, what did you learn about yourself? Write at least one insight.

Flutter Diary

Date _____

Catch the flutter:

Dig more deeply:

Tool 27 PROJECT BIAS REDUCTION

✳ **Purpose:** Increase awareness and understanding of one's own biases

Practice intentional actions and attitudes to reduce your biases

👤 **User(s):** Leaders, teachers

📚 **Leader Resource:**

Building Brilliant Schools by Dr. Andy Parker (2021), Chapters 8 through 10

📝 **Supplies:**

Worksheet E.27a, Bias Expressions and Triggers

Worksheet E.27b, Steps Toward Banishing Bias

Description:

This tool is a self-guide that is informed by research. It offers some advice about actions individuals or groups of educators can take or do to move toward identifying and lessening bias in the school. Some of these ideas have been part of previous tools. Here, a list form is used to identify some behaviors and biases that might be unconscious for teachers, followed by some helpful steps to reduce bias. This tool will be useful to help educators increase awareness and acceptance of pervasive unintentional bias, to keep the topic of bias and bias eradication in mind, and to gather a series of concrete actions that help diminish or erase biases which skew expectations in the school setting.

Steps:

1. Patricia Devine, bias researcher, believes that bias can be found and eliminated. Some of her work was described in Tool 26, Bias Alert! Her bias-intervention workshops are based on the belief that unconscious bias is like a habit that can be reduced through a combination of actions. She's seen evidence of people who grow in confidence that they can overcome their prejudicial habits. Share with the participants these actions for tackling bias:

   • Becoming aware of your own bias;

   • Recognizing and becoming concerned about the effects of bias; and

   • Applying specific strategies to reduce bias (Devine et al., 2012).

2. You, or others in your group, might be wondering whether you indeed do have biases about students, colleagues, parents, or others in the school community. Or, you (or others) might doubt that you actually convey biases (explicit or implicit) to your students or others around you. Share the following thoughts to ponder with participants:

   • Implicit (or unintentional) biases are unconscious. So, it is natural that some of us may not be sure we have them or may not want to think that we do.

   • Biases, conscious or unconscious, do not always lead to overt behaviors.

   • Teachers (and leaders) are often careful not to express biases of which they are aware. Yet we educators, being human, do express biases subtly, unconsciously. And others do pick up on and interpret subtle verbal or nonverbal clues—even young students.

   • Data from samplings of millions of subjects in neuroimaging studies (with MRIs) and from the Implicit Association Test find an extremely high number of responses associated with bias across the board. This leads researchers to conclude that bias is in place and can be measured, even when persons are not aware of it.

   • Researchers Jordan Starck and colleagues (2020) evaluated explicit and implicit bias for a large sample (hundreds of thousands of tests). They found that teachers hold explicit and implicit racial biases in similar percentages as other members of the population.

3. Read the examples on **Worksheet E.27a, Bias Expressions and Triggers**. Take time to consider (and connect to) these examples individually. Or read and discuss them in groups. Follow the instructions on the worksheet to circle those that are your behaviors or biases.

   Subtle Expressions of Bias: Note to participants that
   All of these small cues accumulate to give students messages of optimism or joy (or lack of these), belief or disbelief, and a level (high or low) of confidence in a student's ability.

   Bias Triggers: Note to participants that
   *There are dozens of situations every day in which our biases about students or others are triggered. Though our biases are rooted deeply within our own experiences and influences—they are frequently activated by some characteristic or behavior of an individual. **And most, if not all of these biases, inform and affect expectations about how intellectually capable students are and how they will perform in school.***

4. Review **Worksheet E. 27b, Steps Toward Banishing Bias.** These are all concrete actions that each enable steps toward reducing bias. Together, these actions form a powerful force for an individual—and an even more powerful force when the whole faculty is working on the same steps!

5. Individuals can follow the instructions on Worksheet E.27b. Encourage them to do Steps 1 through 6 in order. The other steps can be done in any order; many of them can and should be done simultaneously.

6. Leaders: Provide time for teachers or leaders to work together on these actions, to discuss their experiences, and to support each other. Facilitate ways for them to practice and connect the steps until they become new habits.

7. Leaders: Be a model of someone taking these actions—applying them to your work with other leaders, with teachers and other staff members, with students, and with parents and community members. Talk about the actions represented in each step. Share your progress. Do them together with colleagues. Ask for help with them. Engage others to support you and give you feedback about your expressions of bias, your triggers, and your progress on the steps shown on Worksheet E.27b.

Bias Expressions and Triggers

These are examples of subtle expressions of bias and some of many characteristics that can trigger our biases—all of this perhaps happening beneath our awareness. These might be approving (or positive) biases or disapproving (or negative) biases. Read them thoughtfully. Circle any that give rise to a flutter of recognition for you.

Subtle Expressions of Bias

a sigh

a head shake (no—or yes)

a diverting of attention

turning away

turning toward

tightening jaw

tightening fists

a tone of voice

a shoulder touch

a smile

a frown

a grimace

a look of relief

a stem face

arms open

arms crossed across chest

OR, a contrast between any one of these in response to one student as compared to other students

Bias Triggers

ethnicity

skin color

gender

gender identity

religion

language

SES (socioeconomic status)

social desirability

social group/friends

appearance

manners

introversion

extraversion

conduct

sexual identity

personality

confidence

politeness

family structure

self-confidence level

clothing or style choices

neatness or lack thereof

hairstyle

body odors

annoying behavior

hygiene matters

habits

language patterns

writing patterns

physical abilities

physical disabilities

participation style

cultural patterns or choices

level of independence

aggressive tendencies

submissive tendencies

organizational skills

seat the student selects

student's track/ability group

cultural patterns or choices

family members' characteristics

sibling performance or behavior

the reputation of previous school student attended

student's perceived "matching up" to the reputation of this school

student history (related by other staff members or passed along in cumulative records)

Take another look at any items you have circled.
Set some goals for what you will do about managing these behaviors and triggers.

Name _____

Steps Toward Banishing Bias

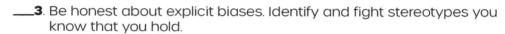

Follow these steps to progress in noticing, acknowledging, and dispelling biases. Review the items weekly. Each time, add a checkmark for those on which you have actively worked or improved since your last reading. Here's looking for lots of checkmarks! ✔

____**1.** Be open to awareness of your biases. Be aware of things that trigger your biases.

____**2.** Work at uncovering your unintentional biases.

____**3**. Be honest about explicit biases. Identify and fight stereotypes you know that you hold.

____**4.** Identify and face the harm that biases can do to others and yourself.

____**5.** Pay attention to others' responses. Look for withdrawal, wincing, sadness, anger, shame—any signs that a bias affects your teaching or relationships, or both, (even if you did not know it existed). This helps you notice your biases.

____**6.** Make your own list of your behaviors that flow from your biases. You need to identify these too, so that you can change them.

____**7.** Eagerly participate in training and discussions with colleagues about implicit bias.

____**8.** As colleagues, work together at helping (not policing) each other to reduce bias. Jointly, name biases and identify ways to change behavior that flows from them.

____**9.** With colleagues, examine and identify biases prevalent in the school community.

____**10.** Practice gratitude and kindness. The more you do this, the more open-hearted and compassionate you will be.

____**11.** Practice an empathetic mindset toward students, especially in matters of discipline.

____**12.** Get to know students and colleagues as individuals. Forming stronger relationships with anyone allows you to drop preconceptions and erroneous assumptions.

____**13.** Be persistent. It will take some students (or adults) longer to trust you.

____**14.** In and out of school, develop cross-group friendships (outside of your usual social groups).

____**15.** Be optimistic. Automatic biases are changeable. We all can learn new **behaviors.**

Tool 28   HIGH-EXPECTATIONS BEHAVIORS

✳ **Purpose:** Identify and practice behaviors known to communicate high expectations to students and help them reach the expectations

👤 **User(s):** Leaders, teachers

📚 **Leader Resource:**

Building Brilliant Schools by Dr. Andy Parker, (2021), Chapters 8 through 10

📝 **Supplies:**

Worksheet E.28, Am I a High-Expectations Teacher?

Description:

Do you behave differently with students you have already decided can succeed (than with those for whom you have lower expectations)? Research shows that many teachers often do. (It's likely that this is true, as well, for leaders in connection with students or even with colleagues.) Teachers' high expectations translate into specific teacher behaviors—communication style, body language, kinds of assignments, resources used, time spent with the student, and feedback. Such behaviors often contribute to accelerated student performance.

In general, teacher expectations influence their own behavior and the resulting performance of students. Researchers Brophy and Good (1970) developed a four-step model to explain how this works: 1) Teacher develops expectations. 2) Teacher treats student differently, according to expectations. 3) Student reacts to teachers' treatment. 4) Student outcomes are improved or limited (pp. 365–366).

Researcher Christine Rubie-Davies and her colleagues have studied the effectiveness of teacher-expectation intervention across a variety of schools, grade levels, genders, ethnicities, and socioeconomic levels. Results showed that when teachers were trained in the practices of high-expectation teachers, student achievement markedly improved, compared to students whose teachers were not trained (Rubie-Davies et al., 2015; Rubie-Davies & Rosenthal, 2016).

High expectations are not enough. To help students achieve at their best, teachers also must

- Believe that all students CAN meet those high expectations;

- Articulate high expectations to students; and

- **Provide the necessary support** to help students reach high expectations.

Steps:

1. Share with participants the information in the Description above. Re-state the final phrase from the previous page, as it is a key idea for Expectations Tool 28: *Teachers must provide the necessary support that students need to reach high expectations.* Researchers have watched what it is that teachers do with or for students for whom they hold high expectations. These identified behaviors are the content of the training teachers received in the studies described on the previous page. And they are the content of our strategy in this tool.

2. Share copies of **Worksheet E.28, Am I a High-Expectations Teacher?** Let participants know that these are behaviors observed in research settings—what teachers do as they work with students for whom they have high expectations (as opposed to students for whom they have lower expectations).

3. Participants follow instructions at the top of the worksheet. Allow time for all individuals to read through the questions and answer each one for themselves. Emphasize the idea that the questions are asking if they do this for ALL students (as opposed to only for students they have already assumed will succeed and can meet high expectations).

4. After thoughtfully reading and responding to each question, participants follow the instruction at the bottom of the page. Once the priorities are ranked, each participant makes a plan for how they will improve in each of those actions.

5. Leaders: Find a time and setting for teachers to share their plans, actions, and progress on their improvement goals. They can choose other priorities when these actions have become habits! Revisit this topic and tool frequently to help these behaviors become habits.

Am I a High-Expectations Teacher?

Your goal is to hold high expectations for ALL—and thus to develop and broaden these behaviors for every one of your students. Check yourself on these proven examples of high-expectations teacher behavior.

1. Ask yourself each question. Then, check the column **Y** (for yes, I am fairly consistent with this) or **N** (not regularly or not at all; I need to do better at this).

Do I do this equally for every student:

Y	N	Priority Rating	Behavior
			Set high expectations from the beginning of a year, class, or task?
			Communicate expectations clearly, verbally and non-verbally?
			Put serious effort into preparing lessons?
			Supply a wide variety and high level of resources?
			Provide a framework for learning?
			Show positive attitude when evaluating the student's work?
			Offer the student many response opportunities?
			Supply the student with challenging instruction?
			Give plenty of positive, constructive feedback?
			Dedicate enough time to answering the student's questions?
			Offer individualized, differentiated instruction and intervention rather than differentiated expectations?
			Use higher-order thinking questions and activities?
			Use scaffolding and other support techniques to help the student learn and reach goals and high expectations?
			Avoid demeaning criticism of the student's work or responses?
			Interact regularly with the student in supportive, caring ways?
			Show that I am devoted every student and to teaching them?
			Encourage the student to have high self-expectations?
			Let parents know I believe the child can meet high expectations?

2. Go back through the list; look at the ones marked **N**.
   Prioritize the top 5 of these (mark 1 through 5) for your first improvement goals.

Tool 29

EXPECTATIONS BY THE BUCKETFUL

⊛ **Purpose:** Build awareness of the copious amounts of expectations in the school setting; identify some of the many expectations, how they are communicated, their clarity or ambiguity, and the equality with which they are applied

User(s): Leaders, teachers

Leader Resource:

Building Brilliant Schools by Dr. Andy Parker (2021), Chapters 8 through 10

Supplies:

Worksheet E.29a, Bucket List (Leader's Guide)

Worksheet E.29b, Anatomy of an Expectation (3 copies for each group)

Buckets (1 per group, 1 for the leader, and a large one for the whole group)

Small cards or paper squares (3 for each person)

Large mural paper pieces—one for each group plus two for the leader

Assortment of markers for each table

Description:

The expectations that teachers hold for their students wield tremendous power in the performance and future success of those students. Beyond teacher expectations for students, all persons in the school community affect and are affected by the expectations we have of one another. These expectations, some of them explicit (outwardly stated) and some of them implicit (unconscious, hidden, or unintentional) fan out to include teachers, all other staff members, school and district leaders, parents and families, and the wider community. This tool engages participants in the process of considering and naming some of many expectations they have for individuals and groups in the school. They work to state and share their expectations—then consider the clarity and reasonableness of the expectations, how they are communicated, and how equitably they are applied.

Steps:

Advance preparation:
- Fasten large mural paper on the walls—one sheet for each group plus two for leader.
- Arrange the room to allow a gathering place for several small groups (at tables or circles of chairs). Place the cards or paper, markers, and a bucket in the center of each table.
- Place one "group" bucket in the center of the room.

Brainstorm, Write, and Read Expectations

1. Do a lightning-quick brainstorm session (about two minutes) where participants name persons involved in expectations in the school (e.g., teachers' expectations of students, students of teachers, teachers of each other, leaders of staff, staff of leaders, teachers of parents, etc.). See Part I on **Worksheet E.29a, Bucket List (Leader's Guide).**

2. Next, choose ONE of those categories for your focus (e.g., leaders' expectations of teachers).

3. Do a quick brainstorm session (about two minutes) around which expectations might fall into that category (e.g., how a job is done, work ethic, academic behaviors, classroom procedures, attendance, relationships, social behavior, discipline, meetings, etc.).

4. Break into small groups of 3 to 5 persons. When settled in groups, follow the guidelines for the activity as described on **Worksheet E.29a, Bucket List (Leader's Guide)**

5. As participants write expectations in the chosen category, **you—the leader, must write, as well**. Place your cards in your own bucket.

6. Give groups about 10 minutes to skim the cards in their own buckets (setting aside duplicates) and place them in the all-group bucket in the center of the room.

Analyze Expectations

7. Drawing from your own (leader's) bucket of the expectations, model an analysis of some expectations. Do not distribute Worksheet E.29b yet, but follow the A-J process on that sheet.

   • Write one of your expectations on your piece of mural paper.

   • State your thinking/answers aloud to each of the questions A-J, and write short answers on the mural. You might wish to enlist participants to help you answer some of those questions about your expectation.

   • Repeat this with another expectation you draw from your bucket.

   • Add your remaining cards to the all-group bucket. Mix the cards well.

8. Each group draws three cards from the all-group bucket.

9. Distribute three copies of **Worksheet E.29b, Anatomy of an Expectation,** for each group.

10. Groups begin by choosing one card and working together to complete the worksheet for that expectation. As time permits, they can do the same for the other two cards drawn.

Share and Discuss Expectations

11. Each group goes to one of the mural papers and writes their names or initials on the paper. The group writes the expectation on a mural, and transfers their answers/thinking/ideas (from Worksheet E.29b) to that paper.

12. Each group shares its work with the whole class, answering questions about it.

13. Use this process as an opportunity to discuss such topics as

    • How to communicate expectations

    • How to clarify expectations (For example, what does it mean "to do your work well" or "to be consistent with your homework" or "to be respectful to peers"?)

    • How ambiguous policies lead to uncertainty

    • How to tell if an expectation is attainable for all

    • How to tell if different students/colleagues are held to an expectation to different levels

    • How to tell if an expectation is logical or necessary

    • How and when to let persons know they've met or not met an expectation

    • How to adapt an expectation if it is unreasonable or not attainable for all

    • How to SHOW, rather than just state, high expectations

    • The reality of unspoken expectations (the "hidden curriculum" of schools)

    • What to do about unspoken expectations or norms

Follow-Up

14. Using copies of Worksheet E.29b, participants can continue to state and analyze expectations **in other categories of expectations**. They can do this individually or with their groups in this session (if time permits) or in other sessions.

15. Encourage participants to use a process such as this to regularly examine and adjust expectations.

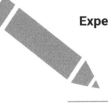

Bucket List (Leader's Guide)

These guidelines will help leaders ignite thinking, sharing, and analysis of some of the many expectations in the school setting. Use the suggestions here to pilot your colleagues through the steps described on the previous pages for Tool 29.

I. List types of expectations to examine.

Expectations you have . . .
1. For your students (academic)
2. For your students (non-academic)
3. For other teachers
4. For support staff
5. For the school leader(s)
6. For students' parents
7. For yourself in your role at school

Expectations you think . . .
8. The school leader has for you
9. Your students have for teachers
10. Are held for all students in the school

II. Agree on a category. With the group, choose one of the 10 expectations categories for the first focus. (Or choose one at random.)

III. Give these instructions:

• Each take 3 cards from your table. Write the category of expectation at the top of each card.

• On each card, write an expectation that comes to your mind (within the focus category).

• Write an expectation this way:
I expect students to _____
Team members expect each other to _____
I think the school leader expects me to _____

• Put your finished cards into the bucket at your table.

IV. Review the cards. Allow time for groups to skim the cards, set duplicates aside, and add their bucketful to the group bucket.

V. Analyze the expectations. To share, analyze, and discuss some of the expectations, follow steps 7 through 13 in the instructions for tool 29.

50 Tools for Building Brilliant Schools, copyright © 2022 by Dr. Andy Parker

Anatomy of an Expectation

Use these questions to guide a close-up examination and analysis of any expectation. Consider each question thoughtfully. Use your answers to direct your future actions. Start by stating the expectation and identifying persons to whom it applies.

I expect _____ to _____
                Who?   **Do What?**

A) How is this expectation communicated?

B) Is it clear? Or ambiguous? Or unspoken? (Circle one.)

C) Is it attainable for all? Or just for some? (Circle one.)

D) Are different people held to this to different levels? Yes   No (Circle one).

E) If so, who's held to what levels?

F) Is this expectation logical and necessary? Yes   No (Circle one)

G) If so, why? If not, why not?

H) How does the person(s) holding the expectation let the others know when they have met this expectation?

I) How does the person(s) holding the expectation let the others know when they have not met this expectation?

J) If ambiguous, unspoken, unattainable for some, unequally applied, or unnecessary—what can I/we do to remedy this expectation's flaws?

Tool 30

REFLECTING ON THE TOOLS

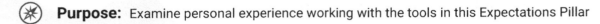

Purpose: Examine personal experience working with the tools in this Expectations Pillar

User(s): Leaders, teachers, students

Leader Resource:

Building Brilliant Schools by Dr. Andy Parker, (2021), Chapters 8 through 10

Supplies:

Worksheet E.30, Looking Back and Looking Forward
A list of the tools that have been used from this chapter
Results of completed tasks from tools in this chapter

Description:

This tool offers a way for those who have used the tools in this section to reflect on what they have done and learned. In addition, it inspires a look forward as to what concepts, behaviors, or goals they will develop and use in the future.

Steps:

1. Distribute copies of **Worksheet E.30, Looking Back and Looking Forward**, as a guide. Also provide a list of the tools that have been used by individuals or groups in their work together. In addition, if the folks reflecting have saved any products or worksheets from the individual tools—these would be helpful to have on hand as participants reflect over their experiences.

2. With the worksheet as a guide, individuals reflect on their own and note their reflections. If students have used some of the tools, you might invite them to do the same or similar process of reflection.

3. Depending on the setting, groups may choose to share and discuss their reflections. Teams or grade-level groups or entire faculties may wish to use the reflections to set goals together.

Name _____

Looking Back and Looking Forward

Reflect on what you learned, thought, experienced, and wish to do further with the tools in this pillar. Write a comment in each category.

Most powerful tool for me, and why	
Most challenging tool for me, and why	
A key idea I learned	
Tool that I think will be great for my students, and why	
Tool that's been most helpful to my group of colleagues, and why	
Something I learned about myself while using these tools	
Two goals I want to set for myself related to the tools in this pillar	

Chapter 4

Tools for Your ACHIEVEMENT Toolbox

There's no elevator to success. You have to take the stairs.

– Unknown

This collection of tools focuses on the beliefs, skills, processes, and practices that have been identified, through good research, as key influences on academic success and on possibilities for all students to reach high levels of achievement.

⚙ Definitions

Achievement:

> *the many steps and stages in a process—fueled by skill, effort, courage, belief in self, support from others, and tenacity— toward and culminating in successfully learning or doing something and in understanding what you did, how you got there, what you learned, and what more you need to learn*

⚙ Key Benefits of Achievement

- The very experience of achieving, itself, yields a wealth of benefits to students—beyond the academic accomplishments. When they see themselves as students having repeated successes with gaining the skills, processes, and content of learning (i.e., achieving), self-belief, self-confidence, and fuller engagement with school all flourish.

- Students with high achievement are more likely to be employed after the school years and to have skills and options for occupations, more stability in jobs, greater confidence in one's work, and higher work-related satisfaction.

- Once students gain the fulfillment and knowledge of successful learning, **they are more likely to have continued academic success.**

- When schools give students excellent instruction and support in meeting high expectations leading to experiences of academic success, students have greater

  - Self-motivation

  - Self-expectations

  - Pro-social inclinations and behavior

  - Quality relationships with teachers and peers

  - Self-control and self-regulation

  - Sense of belonging

  - Willingness to participate

  - Engagement in collaborative activities

  - Goal orientation and goal accomplishment

  - Motivation and pride in their work

  - Academic tenacity

⚙ Influences on Achievement

Here are some of the factors that show up repeatedly as contributing positively to student achievement:

- Student self-evaluation and self-reporting of their progress and processes

- Regular, clear, and meaningful feedback given to students as they learn and work

- High student involvement in and control over their learning

- Focus on goal setting, goal management, and helping individual students reach goals

- Attention to developing conceptual understanding, metacognition, and creativity

- Consistent encouragement of self-belief and self-determination for students

- Frequent use of true cooperative learning

- A commitment to a culturally aware, culturally responsive, and culturally affirming climate, teaching practices, and behaviors

- Regular examination of and diminishing of biases and stereotypes and their effects on individual students or groups of students in the academic processes

- High, clear expectations with measurable goals and benchmarks for achievement

- Focused practices to help students reach expectations

- Skilled, passionate, culturally competent, effective teachers supported by good professional development

- High-quality instruction, with a wide variety of proven instructional strategies

- Challenging and engaging content and active learning experiences that students see as having value, relevance, and connection to their lives

- Ongoing practices to improve curriculum and classroom instruction

- Strong, trusting relationships within the school

- Data-driven decisions throughout the district, school, and classrooms

- Effective, proactive classroom management

- Intentional teaching of SEL skills

- Meaningful involvement of parents and local community

- A safe (physical, social, emotional) environment for learning

- Courageous, collaborative leadership

- A school-wide action plan to raise achievement

- Regular gratitude practice throughout the school community

Note: For a more complete discussion of definitions and benefits of achievement success, as well as influences on achievement and obstacles to achievement, see Chapters 11 through 13 in **Building Brilliant Schools: What G.R.E.A.T. Leaders Do Differently**, by Dr. Andy Parker (2021). Use the next page to keep notes from your reading of those chapters.

⚙ Achievement Tools for Brilliant Schools

Each of the following tools teaches or strengthens one or more of the skills known to nurture higher achievement.

31. Checking Up on Achievement Boosters (Influences on Achievement)

32. Getting to Know SMART Goals (Awareness of Effective Goal Design)

33. SMART Goal Setting for Students (Student Goal-Setting, Metacognition)

34. Meeting SMART Goals (Student Working Plan to Meet Goals)

35. Feedback Tune-Up (Effective Feedback among Colleagues)

36. Do We Hear You? (Checkup on Student Voice)

37. Performance Predictions (Student Self-expectations, Metacognition)

38. Cognitive Task Analysis (Metacognition Skills)

39. Jigsaw Revisited (Collaborative Learning, Metacognition, Critical Thinking)

40. Reflecting on the Tools (Self-Evaluation on Use of Achievement Tools)

Notes from Achievement Chapters

Building Brilliant Schools: What G.R.E.A.T. Leaders Do Differently, Chapters 11–13

As you read about Achievement, jot down key ideas or points that you want to remember from each chapter.

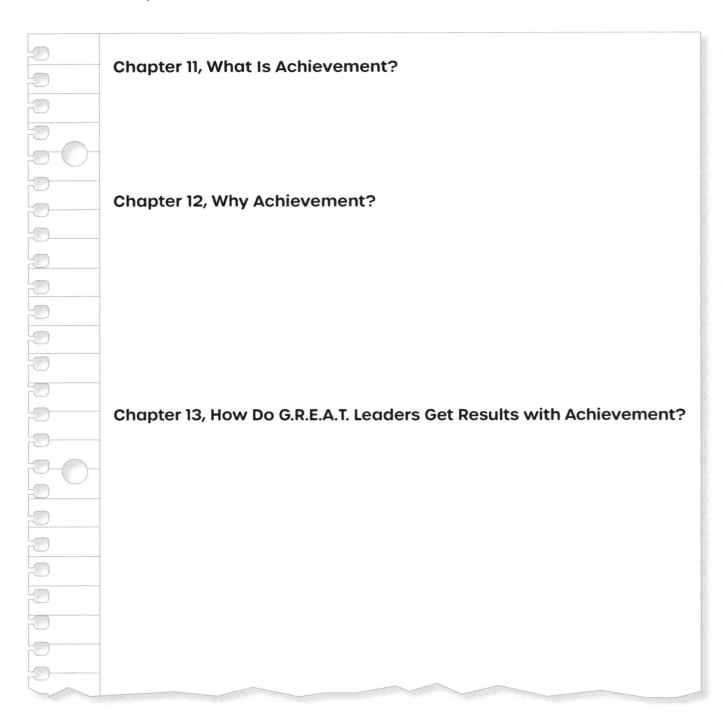

Chapter 11, What Is Achievement?

Chapter 12, Why Achievement?

Chapter 13, How Do G.R.E.A.T. Leaders Get Results with Achievement?

Tool 31

CHECKING UP ON ACHIEVEMENT BOOSTERS

✳ Purpose: Identify influences that boost achievement
Reflect on how well the school (or individual) is practicing/succeeding with these

👤 User(s): Leaders, teachers

📚 Leader Resource:

Building Brilliant Schools by Dr. Andy Parker (2021), Chapters 11 through 13

📝 Supplies:

Worksheet A.31, How Are We Influencing Achievement?

Description:

Decades of research has focused on just how to help all students achieve at the best-possible levels. John Hattie (2008), Professor of Education from New Zealand, has examined large meta-studies to find out what works. With a team of researchers, he scoured the world for evidence of the effectiveness of different teaching methods and interventions. He found that many classroom practices **do** enhance student achievement. But his main interest was to examine what was **most effective**, and he found that about half of the schools/teachers were not consistently doing the most effective things. His work sought out teaching methods that could be verified (with evidence) as effective.

This tool offers a way for leaders and teachers to self-reflect on their own programs—examining them to consider how, and how well, some of the highly-effective influences on achievement are included in the experiences they offer to students.

Steps:

1. Decide on a setting and on group composition for examining your school or classroom achievement interventions and influences (staff meetings, grade-level groups, teams, etc).

2. Share this information about influences on achievement:
   John Hattie's work, based on a massive gathering of data, is called "Visible Learning." This describes the process where teachers and leaders pay attention to the impact of the teaching. **Instead of focusing on how teachers are teaching—focus on how well students are learning.** This means constantly watching, self-evaluating, and adjusting accordingly. The methods Hattie has identified help make learning as visible as possible (2021). He says to **watch students** to see what is working and not working. Watching for struggle, change, or growth, you'll see what is needed **(it will be *visible*)!**

3. You might also share this information from Hattie's book, *Visible Learning for Teachers* (2012). He identifies qualities of teachers that impact student learning the most. Some of those at the top of his list are:

   • Have and show passion about helping their students learn

   • Monitor their impact on students' learning, and adjust their methods accordingly

   • Provide feedback to students about their learning

   • Believe that all students can succeed

   • Are clear about what they want their students to learn (and make this clear to students)

   • Build strong relationships with their students

   • Create an optimal classroom climate for learning

   • Use evidence-based, good teaching practices

   • Actively and consistently seek to improve their own teaching

   • Have, collectively, a strong belief in their ability to positively affect students. (Hattie and his team now label this **collective teacher efficacy** as the new number one influence on student achievement.)

4. Working individually, in pairs, small groups, teams, grade-level gatherings, or other workable combinations, use **Worksheet A.31, How Are We Influencing Achievement?** to reflect on and evaluate how you're doing with these proven methods for raising achievement.

   • Ask yourself/yourselves: *How well do I (we) attend to these as a teacher (or as a staff or school)?* Rate yourself on each item.

   • Consider what evidence shows that you are doing this somewhat, often, or always. Briefly note this evidence.

   • Prioritize what needs your attention. On the worksheet, number the top 5 or 10 things you want to learn about, try, practice, or improve.

5. Take whatever time is needed to discuss this reflection. Share insights and viewpoints. If the evaluation relates to the school or a group, broaden the discussion about what evidence makes the learning visible. What are students showing you by their responses, work, progress, or struggles? Make decisions together on priorities and strategies for improvement.

Name _____

How Are We Influencing Achievement?

Do you have programs or processes that regularly teach, practice, and evaluate these proven, positive influences on student achievement? Rate yourself on how you are doing. For each rating of 3, 4, or 5, briefly describe evidence of use. To the left of the first column, prioritize items (1-5 or 1-10) that you want to work on improving.

Rating Scale: 1 *Never;* **2** *Rarely;* **3** *Sometimes;* **4** *Often;* **5** *Always*

Influence	Rating	Evidence
Collective teacher efficacy		
Prompt, in-process, effective feedback		
Problem-solving skills		
Metacognitive strategies		
Cognitive task analysis		
Students' prediction of their own academic performances		
Setting, managing, and meeting challenging goals		
Students' self-evaluation and reflection		
Students' belief in themselves as learners		
Frequent collaborative learning		
Memory skills (mnemonics)		
Worked examples (demonstrating all steps to do a task)		
Direct instruction to teach specific skills		
Study skills—cross-discipline as well as discipline-specific		
Classroom discussion		
Summarization in all content areas		
Deliberate, spaced practice		
Regular, targeted scaffolding		
Perceived task value (students understand value of a task)		
Work on academic tenacity		
Intentional SEL skills		
Bias awareness and reduction		
Integrated curriculum		
Intrinsic motivation		
Creativity programs; creativity is counted as achievement		
Extracurricular programs (variety, easily accessible to all)		
Strong, trustworthy, collaborative school leaders		
Healthy, proactive school climate		
Availability of counseling; advisory setting for all students		

Tool 32 GETTING TO KNOW SMART GOALS

✳ **Purpose:** Build and practice abilities to design clear, meaningful goals (SMART Goals) that lead to efficient and effective work

👤 **User(s):** Leaders, teachers

📚 **Leader Resource:**

Building Brilliant Schools by Dr. Andy Parker, (2021), Chapters 11 through 13

📝 **Supplies:**

Worksheet A.32a, SMART-Goal Primer
Worksheet A.32b, Are Our Goals SMART?

Description:

As far back as the late 19th century, American philosopher Elbert Hubbard posited that many people failed at various undertakings—not because of grit or low ability—but because they did not organize their efforts around a clear goal (Haughey, 2014). Since that time, multiple studies have found that goal setting and goal management have striking positive effects on productivity and achievement. In 1981, business consultant George Doran and his colleagues developed SMART goals as a way to write management objectives (Doran et al.). Their idea uses the acronym to identify elements of meaningful goals. In the past few decades, this has become a popular base for goal setting in many fields—including education.

This tool, a primer on setting SMART goals, supplies leaders and teachers with a guide for identifying meaningful goals for themselves and for their students. With the tool's worksheets, leaders and teachers use a process for examining their own goals to identify those that are SMART and those that need some help to get smarter!

Steps:

1. Split the group into smaller groups of two or three. Ask them to take pencils/pens and paper with them. Once in groups, dive right into goals! With no introduction to the topic, begin a session with your group of leaders or teachers by asking them to think about goals they have set for their students and themselves. As you identify a type of goal, they'll be asked to write it. Here are some ideas for instructions—but vary these to tailor them to your situation, group makeup, grade levels, etc. Group members work together to write the following goal types:

- **Goals 1:** Write a goal you have set recently for your class for an academic task, project, process, or other desired accomplishment.

- **Goal 2:** Write a goal you have set for an individual in your class for an academic task, project, process, or other desired accomplishment.

- **Goal 3:** Write a goal you have set for yourself related to your teaching (e.g., a strategy to use, a new skill to gain, a unit you will prepare, something you will change, etc.)

2. Hold a brainstorming session or conversation with your group to share what you already know and have experienced about goals—what they include and how they are written. (At this point, focus only on the stating of the goal itself.) This is a way to get an idea of what approaches teachers in your group **have already used** to set and measure goals.

3. Distribute copies of **Worksheet A.32a, SMART-Goal Primer.** Many leaders and teachers will already be familiar with SMART goals, so this will be a review. (However, some may not have studied this in depth.) Take time for individuals to read this. Talk through it briefly together.

4. Distribute copies of **Worksheet A.32b, Are Our Goals SMART?** Groups examine the goals they just wrote to see how well each one meets requirements of SMART goals. They can suggest ideas for how to adapt or expand goals as needed to make them "smarter."

5. Allow time for groups to share with other groups some of what they found, what they learned, and what they did to adapt goals.

6. Let participants know this: According to its creator, George Doran, the SMART acronym was not intended to be rigid. Over time, the acronym has been modified. And different users and writers have different "takes" on the acronym. The R was originally for "realistic," but is also used now as "relevant" or "rigorous" or both. Some have added ER to call the goals SMARTER—E for evaluated (using a process for monitoring the goal and assessing the extent and quality to which it has been met), and R for reviewed (using a process for reflecting, examining, and adapting **during** the work toward the goal).

7. Groups or individuals can use Worksheets A.32a and A.32b to examine other goals. Encourage all teachers to use a SMART-Goal model when planning goals. They can use Tools 33 and 34 to teach the model to students and to help students design and meet their own goals.

SMART-Goal Primer

Use this overview of the SMART-Goals model as you consider and design goals for individuals, groups, or yourself and as you teach students to create their goals.

Specific	The goal should be clear and precise about what is to be accomplished. In setting a goal, learners might consider not only what to accomplish but also why the goal is important, who will be involved, where the goal will be worked on or completed, and which materials or resources are involved or needed.
Measurable	The goal must be something that can be measured. This will include mini-goals or steps that can be reached along the way, in order to break the work into manageable segments and make it easier to track the progress. This part of the goal will answer such questions as *How much? How many? and What will accomplishment or final performance look like?*
Achievable	A goal must be attainable and realistic. It must be limited enough to attain within the time, resources, and constraints involved. In deciding if a goal is attainable, consider what new skills, attitudes, or viewpoints are necessary to work toward and attain the goal.
Relevant and **R**igorous	People need to know that an activity, quest, or task is important. To determine relevance, ask *Why?* The goal must fit within the topic, be of interest to the student, and make sense. A learner needs to know that working for this goal will make a difference. When goals are relevant (they matter, and they connect with a learner's interests or needs), students will be more motivated to meet them. Also, goals that are rigorous motivate and inspire learners to work harder and keep learners engaged. So, the goal should challenge and stretch the learner, but not be so difficult as to be impossible to reach.
Time-related	The goal must be do-able within a reasonable time frame. Time might be dictated by the class time, specific assignment, grade level, or individual learning needs. Students should know clear time parameters before they finalize the goal, so that the amount of work needed can fit into the time frame. Set intermediary time goals for parts of the task, as well as identify a final target date.

50 Tools for Building Brilliant Schools, copyright © 2022 by Dr. Andy Parker

Name(s) _____

Are Our Goals SMART?

Write each goal. Answer Yes or No for each question. For YES answers, use Column 3 to tell how you know you can answer YES. For NO answers, use Column 4 to tell what can be done to change that NO to a YES!

1 Goal:

	Y/N	How?	How will you change it?
Specific?			
Measurable?			
Achievable?			
Relevant and **R**igorous			
Time-related			

2 Goal:

	Y/N	How?	How will you change it?
Specific?			
Measurable?			
Achievable?			
Relevant and **R**igorous			
Time-related			

3 Goal:

	Y/N	How?	How will you change it?
Specific?			
Measurable?			
Achievable?			
Relevant and **R**igorous			
Time-related			

Tool 33
SMART GOAL SETTING FOR STUDENTS

✳ **Purpose:** Teach students to set meaningful goals

👤 **User(s):** Leaders, teachers, students

📚 **Leader Resource:**

Building Brilliant Schools by Dr. Andy Parker (2021), Chapters 11 through 13

📝 **Supplies:**

Worksheet A.33, Get SMART About Goals

Mural paper, posterboard, or tape to create a goal post

A good supply of sticky notes—a bit larger than the normal size, if possible

Description:

When we look at the research into what positively influences student achievement, goal setting shows up high on the list! Goal setting and management are strongly associated with higher achievement. When students are able to set and monitor their own goals, they become more engaged in their work, more aware of the processes of their work, and more invested in doing it. If there is no game plan that leads one toward achieving a goal, work becomes less effective and efficient. The bottom line is this: we need to teach our students to be smart goal setters!

Armed with understandings about setting effective goals (See Tool 32), Tool 33 helps teachers introduce students to SMART goals and guides them in designing their own goals.

Steps:

Note: The steps are written for students to write and revise goals. Leaders and teachers can use the same process for their own goals.

1. Create a goalpost on a wall, whiteboard, or door. Use suggested materials (or others you choose). Put it in a place where students can stick notes above and below it.

2. Brainstorm about goals: Ask students what a goal is. Listen to some impromptu answers. Ask students to name a goal they have or that someone might have. Give the group a few minutes to share ideas.

3. Have students join in pairs. Give each pair about 8 sticky notes. Give these directions:

  • Think of goals that a student could set for schoolwork. Maybe this is a goal for achieving at their best or raising quiz scores or being ready for a certain test or anything else that has to do with doing academic work.

  • Write two such goals—each on a different note. Include the time you think it would take to meet the goal. Write the goals clearly enough so that anyone else can read them.

  • Now, think of goals a student could set for something other than school work. These could be about things at school (relationships, behavior, after-school activities). OR these could be about out-of-school things a student would like to learn, do, or achieve.

  • Write two such goals—each on a different note. Write clearly, and include the time.

4. Students then stick the first two goal notes above the crossbar of the goalpost and the second two below the bar; students return to their seats as pairs.

5. Provide each pair with two copies of **Worksheet A.33, Get SMART About Goals.** Introduce them to the SMART acronym. They won't write on the worksheet yet, but can use the left column for reference. Talk through each component; brainstorm about how they would get a goal to meet the requirements (for example, how to make it specific or measurable). Use some examples from the goalpost; examine how they stack up against the SMART components.

6. Next, students go back to the goalpost, a few pairs at a time, and randomly choose one sticky note from each group (those above and below the goalpost). (*Note:* If any pair finds a goal that they are not able to read or understand, they can go back to choose a replacement.)

7. Choosing one goal and working as if this were their own goal, pairs follow the instructions on the worksheet to analyze the goal and revise it as needed. If time permits, they can repeat this process with the second goal.

8. Provide some time for students to share in larger groups (or whole group) what they found, what they did, and what they learned.

9. Use this process and worksheet again for students to practice writing their own personal SMART goals for actual assignments or projects.

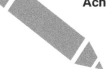

Get SMART About Goals

Write your goal. Answer the questions that will help you decide if it has all the elements of a SMART goal. If the process of answering the questions lets you know that your goal is not quite right—then change it to make it a SMARTER goal!

SMART Goal-Setting Guide for Students	
Name(s):	**Date:**
Write the goal. *Time frame for completing goal:*	

Now, make sure your goal is SMART. Does it include explanation or elements that allow you to answer **yes** to each question? If not, make notes about what the goal needs.

Specific Statement of Goal *Does it tell precisely what you intend to learn or do?*	
Measurable? *Does the goal statement include what the outcome will be or how you will know when you've reached the goal?*	
Achievable? (but a little challenging) *Is it manageable enough to get materials you need and learn the skill or do the task in the time you have?*	
Relevant and **R**igorous *Are you sure about why this goal matters to you?* *Will it stretch you to do or learn something that takes work? (That is, is the goal beyond just easy for you?)*	
Time *Will you be able to do this in the time you have?*	
Use your answers and notes to make revisions needed to make a SMART goal.	
Write the revised goal. *Time frame for completing goal:*	

Tool 34 MEETING SMART GOALS

 Purpose: Create workable plans for moving toward and meeting goals

 User(s): Leaders, teachers, students

Leader Resource:

Building Brilliant Schools by Dr. Andy Parker (2021), Chapters 11 through 13

Supplies:

Worksheet A.34, Getting to My Goals

Description:

This tool is for use by students (or any other goal setters) to make a plan to work toward one of their goals. It teaches them to break the process into manageable, sequential steps that will lead to learning the skill or content they intend to accomplish.

Note: This is intended to be used in conjunction with Achievement Tools 32 and 33 and use of Worksheets A.32a, A.32b, and A.33, which focus on the design and setting of goals

Steps:

Note: The steps are written for students to plan work toward meeting goals. Leaders and teachers can use the same process for their own goals and work plans.

1. Distribute copies of **Worksheet A.34, Getting to My Goals.** Look through it together with students, explaining each part.

2. Choose an example of a goal to demonstrate the use of this worksheet. Do this on a device that allows you to project the worksheet as it is completed. Select a goal that is relevant to work students are doing or will be doing. Students can help you choose the goal.

3. With students contributing ideas for each part, complete the worksheet.

4. If students are new to this type of process, practice the planning before they do it themselves on actual goals they will pursue. Use goals students wrote when using a previous tool, wrote for Tools 32 or 33, or any other well-written goal. Students can work in pairs to complete the worksheet (A.34) again, using goals you suggest or the ones they wrote for Tools 32 or 33, or any other well-written goal.

5. Once students feel comfortable with this planning process, they can use it again and again as work to meet their SMART goals.

Name _____

Getting to My Goals

Write your goal. Then write the steps, in sequence, that you will follow to meet it. Be sure to include target dates for steps, resources needed, and help you will seek.

Plan for Meeting My Goal		
Name:		**Today's Date:**

My Goal Write your specific goal. Include a statement of how you will know when you reach it. Intended completion date or time:	

Steps to Meet My Goal		**Finish Date**
1		
2		
3		
4		
5		
6		

Resources, materials, or locations I need		
Help I need from others Name and tell what you need from each person.	Name	Need
	Name	Need
Reviewers Your teacher and another person to give feedback on your work	Name	
	Name	

Tool 35

FEEDBACK TUNE-UP

✳ **Purpose:** Practice effective feedback among leaders and teachers

👤 **User(s):** Leaders, teachers

📚 **Leader Resource:**

> *Building Brilliant Schools* by Dr. Andy Parker (2021), Chapters 11 through 13

📝 **Supplies:**

> Worksheet A.35a, My Feedback to Colleagues: A Reflection
> Worksheet A.35b, Feedback Practice
> Worksheet A.35c, How I Receive Feedback: A Reflection

Description:

Extensive studies and meta-analyses of studies on student achievement repeatedly identify feedback as one of the top influences that can positively affect student performance. But the effective use of feedback begins with the adults in the school setting. Leaders and teachers must know how to do it well, what works and what doesn't (or even hinders), how it affects the recipient, and what should be done with the feedback once it is received. Educators learn best about feedback when we receive and practice it with each other.

This tool is for leaders and teachers for work on their feedback to each other. The worksheets lead teachers and leaders in exercises to reflect on their current style of giving and receiving feedback and to practice some effective feedback statements. (In the next chapter on Tenacity, you'll find a tool (Tool 48) focused on guidance for teacher feedback to students and peer-to-peer feedback.)

Steps:

1. With leader(s) and teachers working together, introduce the topic of feedback among the educators in the school. Break into small groups to discuss these questions—from a viewpoint of what is not happening, or what could or should happen. Groups should take notes and gather key ideas in response to the questions:

    What is your definition of feedback?
    What does feedback among colleagues look like or sound like?
    What is the purpose of feedback among leaders and teachers? (Why would you do this?)
    After feedback is given/received, what does/should one (or the group) do with feedback?

2. Gather back together with the whole group. Each small group can share some of their answers or ideas. Notice the commonalities. Notice ideas that are not being used now, but could be used. Notice reservations about the feedback process.

3. Back in small groups, discuss these questions:

   What kind of feedback is helpful, useful? and What kind is NOT helpful, useful?
   What kind of feedback do you need from your leader(s)?
   What kind of feedback do you need from fellow teachers (or teammates, etc.)?
   What can be done to overcome reservations about feedback among colleagues?

4. Next, use **Worksheet A.35a, My Feedback to Colleagues: A Reflection,** as an individual self-check. Individuals can add other statements to the list—ideas gleaned from their group discussions.

5. Giving feedback that is specific, kind, respectful, affirmative, and that informs next steps has to do with the language we use. After some time alone with the worksheet, individuals or pairs can practice some feedback language. Use **Worksheet A.35b, Feedback Practice**, for this. Or, as an alternative, participants can cut large "speech bubbles" from paper, write on them, and post them on walls for sharing. For this feedback practice, first identify a typical task or process—something in which leaders and teachers would observe another in some kind of "doing." It can have to do with academic work, collaborative group work, handling problems—anything reasonable. Either the facilitator can name a task for all participants to use, or individuals can each decide a task for their own worksheet feedback practice.

6. Allow time to discuss the feedback-practice process—identifying what was learned and sharing good ideas with one another.

7. Use **Worksheet A.35c, How I Receive Feedback: A Reflection,** at any point in this process. This offers individuals a chance to ponder the ways they receive and use feedback.

8. Emphasize (and implement) the concept of collective work and agreement on feedback practices--doing it regularly (during the process as well as after), having consistent approaches, making use of the feedback, giving feedback about how the feedback was helpful or not, and continually reflecting on how you're doing and how to do it well. Agree on some processes you will use for colleague-to-colleague feedback

My Feedback to Colleagues: A Reflection

Consider each of these questions to help you think about your general style and content in giving feedback to your leaders, team members, or other colleagues. Give a brief answer or comment for each of these questions.

Do I do this?	
Give feedback at all (or rarely?)	
Give straightforward, honest feedback	
Give subtle, or nonverbal feedback (indications of approval, non-approval, affirmation or disaffirmation)	
Give feedback right away	
Give feedback during a process—not just at the end	
Give specifics, stating exactly what went well, what was powerful, what was missing, what was confusing, etc.	
Always include in my feedback what was done well	
Give constructive feedback, relating what was done in relationship to original criteria or goal	
Give feedback that informs next steps—suggestions, alternatives connected to the feedback input	
Give feedback kindly, respectfully	
Give non-arrogant feedback	
Give feedback privately, when appropriate	
Ask for feedback on my feedback	
Notice that the receiver feels comfortable and affirmed with my feedback, and knows what to do next	

Other questions:

Leaders, do you ask for feedback from teachers?

Why. . . or . . . Why not?

Teachers do you ask for feedback from leaders?

Why. . . or . . . Why not?

Name _____

Feedback Practice

Identify a process, task, or situation that poses (or has posed) an opportunity for feedback. This can be real or hypothetical (but representative of something that happens in the school setting). For each example, **write 1 or 2 feedback statements** to fit each description shown. Take care to make all statements kind, honest, and humble. This can be feedback during or after a task. Don't use any specific names.

Who will be the giver of feedback? (Leader, teacher, other)

Who will be the receiver of the feedback? (Leader, teacher, other)

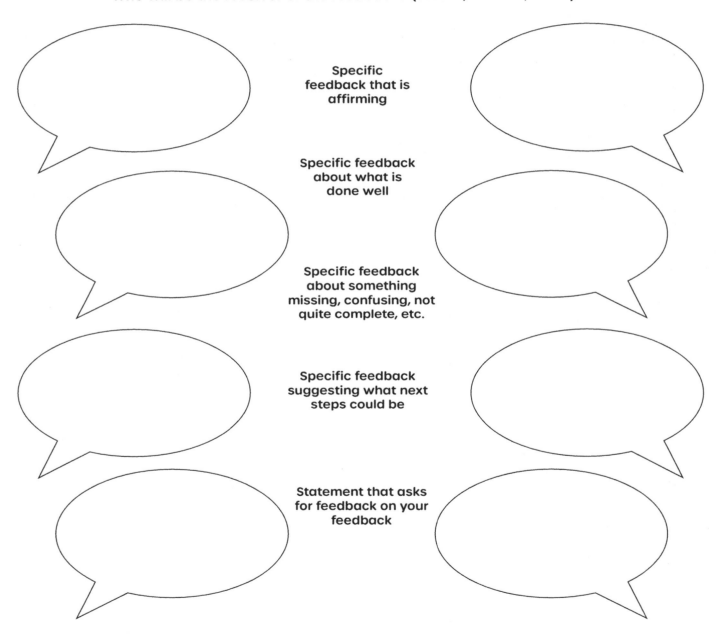

Specific feedback that is affirming

Specific feedback about what is done well

Specific feedback about something missing, confusing, not quite complete, etc.

Specific feedback suggesting what next steps could be

Statement that asks for feedback on your feedback

Name _____

How I Receive Feedback: A Reflection

Consider ideas, needs, attitudes, and feelings as you reflect on your experiences of receiving feedback, particularly from other adults within the school setting. Don't use any specific names in your answers.

1. I do (or do not) want regular feedback from leaders. Here's why:

2. I do (or do not) want regular feedback from team members or other colleagues. Here's why:

3. I'd rate the usefulness of past feedback from leaders as

4. I'd rate the usefulness of past feedback from colleagues as

5. Some of the most valuable feedback I've received was about
   This feedback was given to me by
   Here's what I did with that feedback:

6. I've been grateful for feedback when

7. The worst experience(s) I've had with feedback were

8. When I am given feedback, here is what I usually do with it:

9. If we are to have regular feedback from leaders or colleagues, it should be related to these traits, behaviors, or kinds of tasks:

10. Something that would help me be more comfortable with feedback is

---

Answer these questions:

Leaders: What kinds of feedback do you need from teachers?

Teachers: What kinds of feedback do you need from leaders?

Teachers: What kinds of feedback do you need from students?

---

50 Tools for Building Brilliant Schools, copyright © 2022 by Dr. Andy Parker

Tool 36

DO WE HEAR YOU?

⊛ **Purpose:** Examine school and classroom processes and climate for encouraging, listening to, and learning from students' voices

👤 **User(s):** Leaders, teachers, students

📚 **Leader Resource:**

Building Brilliant Schools by Dr. Andy Parker, (2021), Chapters 11 through 13

📝 **Supplies:**

Worksheet A.36a, Student Voice: Current Practices (Leader and Teacher Survey)
Worksheet A.36b, Is Your Voice Heard? (Student Survey)

Description:

"Student voice" can be defined as the extent to which students are free, able, and invited to express their opinions and viewpoints, ask questions, share themselves, and have a say in the processes of their learning. Research has shown that students who feel engaged, motivated, involved in classroom processes, powerful in charting their academic courses, and worthwhile as learners have increased chances of achieving well. Soliciting student input; teaching them how to voice their ideas, beliefs, and insights; and listening to what they say are all powerful processes for boosting student achievement in all areas of school.

This tool uses two survey activities to assess current practices on student voice and to learn about what might be changed, improved, or established.

Steps:

Note: The steps focus on a process to learn more about boosting student voice in the school and in classrooms. Leaders and teachers can follow a similar process to examine how well the voices of staff members are invited, listened to, developed, and honored in the school. Modify the surveys to focus on that area of "Voice" in the school.

1. Start by involving the group of educators (leaders included) in reflecting on the current practices regarding student voice. Participants can think about this as it pertains to their individual classrooms, or they can work together in pairs or small groups to address the topic as it pertains to team-wide or school-wide practices and plans. Use **Worksheet A.36a, Student Voice: Current Practices**, to guide their thinking and record responses. Participants should feel free to add items to add items to the list.

2. Follow this with discussion and sharing of some of the responses. Perhaps ask such questions as:

> *How would we define "student voice"?*
> *What do we now do that seems common across classes or grade levels?*
> *What ratings surprised us?*
> *What seem to be the strongest or most successful (current) practices?*
> *What might be missing from this list?*

3. The survey asks how often these "indications" of student voice are practiced. But it does not ask how. Start collecting lists of specific practices that individuals, teams, or the school does to honor and develop student voice. That is, what evidence can you give of those attitudes and practices identified as those you now hold or do?

4. Now it's time to gather feedback from students. How does what the educators perceive line up with what the students experience? Use **Worksheet A.36b, Is Your Voice Heard?** to hear from students on this topic. Let students know that this is an anonymous survey.

5. Gather teachers and leaders together again to share what they've learned from the student responses. Compare student impressions and experiences to what the teachers and leaders perceived about student voice in the classroom or school.

6. Use the information gathered from teachers, leaders, and students to expand the discussion of how student voice is defined, viewed, and addressed in your classrooms and school. Come to agreements about what is going well and should be continued. Set times and places to gather other ideas for boosting student voice and to set goals.

7. Make and execute a clear plan for responding to what students told you in their survey. Set goals and dates for acting on factors, practices, and behaviors that need action.

> *In discussions about student voice, remember this: We don't **give** voice to students. Each one already has a voice. What we can give in schools is honor and respect to the validity and worth of their voices and opportunities for voices to be heard. We can listen to them and take them seriously. And we can open ourselves to learn from—and act on—what students have to tell us.*

Class (or Team, School) _____

Student Voice: Current Practices

Rate your individual, team, class or school practices in areas of Student Voice. Use the rating scale 1 to 5. Be ready to identify evidence of those practices that you rate with a 3, 4, or 5.

Rating Scale: 1 *Never;* **2** *Rarely;* **3** *Sometimes;* **4** *Often;* **5** *Regularly*

	Practices	Raitings
1	Students have input in the design, implementation, and evaluation of classroom policies and procedures.	
2	Students have input in the design, implementation, and evaluation of school policies and procedures.	
3	Students are given responsibility in managing classroom procedures.	
4	Students are involved in goal-setting, management, and evaluation.	
5	Students have a say in their own learning (learning goals, goal attainment, learning outcomes, in-class assignments, group project tasks, homework assignments).	
6	Students are invited to speak or write their opinions, feedback, ideas, and questions about daily matters in the classroom and school.	
7	Students have opportunities to explain and demonstrate their learning progress.	
8	Students are offered ways to reflect on what they've learned and how they are progressing.	
9	Students are offered surveys or other ways to share reflections, opinions, evaluations, and ideas anonymously and safely.	
10	Student interaction/expression is a part of all or most lessons.	
11	Discussion is a standard learning strategy.	
12	Collaborative learning and collaborative research are standard strategies.	
13	Students are used as "expert witnesses" in teaching and learning.	
14	We (I) really listen to student input.	
15	We (I) honor and act on student input and feedback.	

Is Your Voice Heard?

The purpose of this survey is for students to share their opinions and experiences about how their voices (opinions, ideas, insights, questions, expressions) are heard and valued in the classroom and school. Rate each item with a check in one box.

	Practices	Rarely or Never	Sometimes	Often	Always
1	The teacher asks for student opinions and ideas.				
2	All students take part in decisions about classroom policies and procedures.				
3	There are many chances and ways for students to take part in decisions about school policies and procedures.				
4	Students are asked to evaluate events, assignments, and projects.				
5	Students are trusted with classroom responsibilities.				
6	I feel safe to express my thoughts freely.				
7	Everyone has many chances to be heard without being afraid or uncomfortable.				
8	I am included in sessions to set goals for my work.				
9	I have a say in my assignments, projects, and homework assignments—in what I do and in how I do it and share it.				
10	All students get lots of chances to share what we learn and show what we know.				
11	I have lots of chances to ask questions.				
12	I feel my questions are taken seriously and answered.				
13	We have student-led conferences.				
14	My voice is listened to, respected, and valued.				
15	The teacher acts on students' suggestions and reflections.				

Tool 37

PERFORMANCE PREDICTIONS

✳ **Purpose:** Students

👤 **User(s):** Leaders, teachers, students

📚 **Leader Resource:**

Building Brilliant Schools by Dr. Andy Parker, (2021), Chapters 11 through 13

📝 **Supplies:**

Worksheet A.37, I Predict!

Description:

Performance prediction is the process of thinking about and stating how someone expects they will perform on an upcoming task or assessment. When paired with follow-up explanation and examination of their predictions plus identification of what they can do to go beyond the prediction—this practice has a strong, positive influence on achievement.

This tool teaches leaders, teachers, and students how to gain the fullest possible benefits from performance predictions. And by the way, this is great practice in metacognition, as well.

Steps:

Note: The steps are written for students to predict their performances. Leaders and teachers can use the same process for predictions about their own performances.

Before the task, assignment, or assessment:

1. Students look over a summary or outline of what an upcoming assessment will cover or what a new task will be. Such a summary or outline provides them with an overview of the content they should know or understand or the task they will perform.

2. Give students a clear idea of what the purpose of the assessment or task is. That is, when finished, what should they know, be able to do, or have completed well?

3. Have students think about what skills or knowledge they will need in order to do the assessment or task. For example, if the test involves finding areas of geometric figures, they must realize that they'll need to know certain geometric formulas. If the task involves displaying data, they'll need to have ideas about how to do that. If the task involves using materials in a lab to do an experiment, they might identify that they need to know the steps of inquiry, safety procedures in the lab, and how to use lab equipment.

4. When students understand the scope of a test, task, or assignment, distribute copies of **Worksheet A.37, I Predict!** Ask them to make a prediction about how they will do on the test, task, or assignment. As part of the prediction, they'll write some comments that explain the why of their prediction. They might make such comments as, *I'm not too confident about choosing the right strategy to solve a problem*, or *I've studied the plant processes well or I don't understand the structure of an essay too well*, or *I've done well on previous math assignments where I needed to find areas of figures*.

5. Pay attention to students' predictions. Hold a discussion about what they might do before the test or during the task to address some of the weaknesses or needs—lack of information, insecurity with a skill, confusion about a concept. This gives them a chance to brush up on something, and it gives you (the teacher) a chance to identify what you can do to help them polish a skill. This is the opportunity to push them beyond their prediction. As they think about what they can and can't do, what they need, what the task or test entails—they are really delving deeper into the material. They are breaking down the challenge into its parts and closely examining their readiness. Because they've seen an overview and know what a good performance will look like—they will be more motivated to reach higher. And since they've dissected the test scope or the task—they will know what it takes to perform well. This process raises their own confidence and expectations as they go into the task, assignment, or test.

After the task, assignment, or assessment:

6. Once they do the task or the test, students compare their predictions to the actual performance. Use the worksheet (A.37), again for them to note how they did on the task and comment about the comparisons.

7. Take time to discuss these comparisons and about what happened between the time they made the prediction and looked at the outcome.

I Predict!

Use this sheet to predict your performance on a task, assignment, or test.
After the task, compare your outcomes with your original prediction.

Before the task, assignment, or test:

The task is _____
_____
_____
_____

On this task, I predict that I will _____
_____
_____

Here's **why** I made this prediction: _____
_____
_____

What I need to do or know to do well on this task: _____
_____
_____

After the task, assignment, or test:

Here's how I did:

How this compares to my prediction:

My comments on this comparison:

What I learned from doing the performance prediction:

Tool 38 COGNITIVE TASK ANALYSIS

⁂ **Purpose:** Increase metacognitive skills by analyzing the cognitive processes used in various parts of doing a task

👤 **User(s):** Leaders, teachers, students

📚 **Leader Resource:**

Building Brilliant Schools by Dr. Andy Parker (2021), Chapters 11 through 13

📝 **Supplies:**

Worksheet A.38, Thinking About Thinking
Large mural paper, markers, tape

Description:

Most educators have plenty of experience practicing breaking a big task down into smaller, manageable steps—and in teaching students how to do this. It's an important skill and process for understanding the components of a task, for evaluating process along the way, and for getting to goals. But how often do we go back and think about what we were actually thinking when we attacked and completed each of those steps?

Notice that this tool is not called "Task Analysis." It is called "Metacognitive Task Analysis." In this process, the student (of any age) purposely examines each sub-task or step of a larger task to notice **what cognitive skills or processes** are needed (or were used) to accomplish that sub-task. This is metacognition that we all can practice regularly. It not only helps you see the parts of a task (of any size). It also helps you analyze how you perform them. It leads to better understanding of how we learn and how amazing and numerous are our cognitive skills!

Leaders, teachers, and students can all use this tool to practice thinking about how they think.

Steps:

Note: Wherever the word "student" is used in these steps, know that it refers to anyone of any age or "job" that is using the process.

1. Discuss metacognition with your group. Present it as a marvelous ability of your own brain—that it is able to analyze and recognize its own processes!

Achievement Tool 38, continued

2. Choose a task. The best introduction to metacognitive task analysis is to demonstrate a task to your "audience." Many different kinds of tasks will work. Choose something interesting to your audience. For example, use an equation to solve a wacky math problem; make a decision about what kind of a car to buy; create steps for how you'll memorize something; follow a recipe to make a milkshake; create a plan you will follow to break a habit or otherwise change a behavior; design a behavior contract for an adolescent; make a plan for how you are going to win an argument with a friend; tell about a relationship issue you worked through; build a simple gingerbread house or birdhouse; work out an action plan for an upcoming all-school Bingo Night or dance party; teach someone to do a particular dance or spin a Hula hoop, etc . . .

3. Working on a large mural or whiteboard surface on the wall, or on a device where work is shown on a screen, write the steps you will follow. Then write or draw what is needed to show how you do the steps.

4. Next, go back through the task. Ask students to think with you to identify one or more cognitive skills needed to do each part or step. Or, if it was something you were planning to do—identify cognitive skills you would need to follow or accomplish the plan. At this point, students could use **Worksheet A.38, Thinking About Thinking**, to follow along and write ideas. OR, you could project the worksheet and complete it (maybe with the help of a student assistant). This step gives a wonderful opportunity to teach or review students' understanding of various thinking skills and processes at various levels of complexity—such skills as

Remembering	*Applying knowledge to a new situation*	*Experimenting*
Accessing prior knowledge	*Demonstrating*	*Questioning*
Memorizing	*Interpreting*	*Problem solving*
Comprehending	*Inferring*	*Decision making*
Classifying, sorting	*Predicting*	*Synthesizing*
Describing	*Drawing conclusions*	*Evaluating/judging*
Explaining	*Analyzing*	*Arguing, defending*
Defining	*Organizing*	*Creating*
Estimating	*Comparing and contrasting*	*Designing*

5. After demonstrating the process, send students off in pairs to select a task of their own, identify the steps, and analyze to notice the cognitive processes needed for each step. You or students can use Worksheet A.38 again and again for tasks of many different kinds!

Name _____

Thinking About Thinking

In the center brain shape briefly describe the task. Next, write the steps (or sub-tasks) in order in the top parts of the numbered bubbles. Use the bottom part of each bubble to name one or more cognitive skill(s) or process(es) needed to accomplish that sub-task.

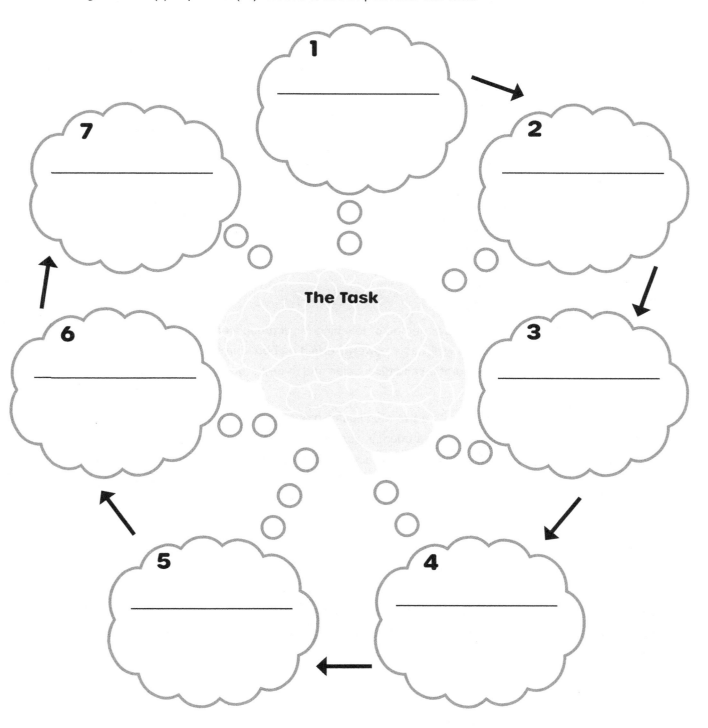

Tool 39

JIGSAW REVISITED

⊛ **Purpose:** Identify metacognitive and collaborative skills through use of the "complete" (three-step) jigsaw learning method

👤 **User(s):** Leaders, teachers

📚 **Leader Resource:**

Building Brilliant Schools by Dr. Andy Parker, (2021), Chapters 11 through 13

📝 **Supplies:**

Worksheet A.39a, Putting the Pieces Together
An assignment topic and plans for dividing the topic into sub-categories
Space for students to meet in groups of four
Jigsaw puzzle pieces (prepared by leader; see Step 1 on page 165)
Markers, tape

Description:

Educators have been using the jigsaw method of teaching (or of group learning) for many years. Research has shown that this method, used well, has a powerful effect on boosting student achievement. It is a wonderful way to promote collaboration and discussion and to give students (of any age) responsibilities for teaching ideas to others.

Most educators are likely familiar with a two-step jigsaw process where students are divided into small, "home" groups. Within that group, each student is assigned to read or learn about one part (or sub-category) of a larger piece of material or topic. Each student has the job to become an "expert" on that part. After doing the assigned task, students gather with other "experts" on that same subcategory to discuss the topic. Eventually, students return to their home groups and each teach the home group about their piece of the "puzzle."

But true jigsaw, as developed in 1971 by its originator Elliot Aronson, goes beyond the often-used two-step process (*Jigsaw Classroom*, 2022). The third step is crucial for practicing critical thinking, for metacognition, and for arriving at deeper understandings about the whole assignment (all the subcategories together). This tool provides leaders and teachers with a way to practice the true three-step jigsaw learning process—gaining all the benefits just mentioned. Having used it themselves, educators can then teach their students the whole of the jigsaw method.

Steps for Guiding the Jigsaw Process:

Note: *The steps are written for teachers to use to guide the Jigsaw Process Steps on page 166 with students. For leaders working with teachers, follow the same process—considering your staff as the students in this practice. Use an assignment that is something the teachers or other adult participants need to learn.*

1. Advance preparation: If you want to give students the option to write some of their analyses and understandings from Step 3 of the process on large puzzle pieces, prepare two or three of these ahead of time for each small group.

2. Choose a task for the class. This can be a reading passage or other content-area task that can be divided into segments. It could be an article to read, a concept or process to learn, a graph to interpret, information about different kinds of erosion to explore, different news reports of the same event, a poem to analyze, a visual performance to analyze (dance, painting, etc.). The idea is that the task/topic must be able to be divided into subcategories or subtopics or sub-tasks—preferably about four.

3. Assign students to Home Groups—preferably four to a group. The number of groups and number of people in a group depend on the number of subcategories of the main assignment/topic. While students are in Home Groups, introduce all groups to the big topic for the whole assignment. Note that each Home Group will get the same set of subtopics.

4. Let students know that each person in the group will have a separate part (or subtopic) of the whole topic to learn about. It will be their jobs to become experts in that topic.

5. Assign each student to an Expert Group. Provide each with the assignment for the part they'll explore (become an expert on).

6. Guide students through the following Jigsaw Process Steps on page 166. Allow as much time as you determine they need as they work through each step.

Jigsaw Process Steps:

Students can use **Worksheet A.39, Putting the Pieces Together**, to write their ideas and notes for each of the three steps.

Step 1: Expert Groups:

Students move from Home Groups to their Expert Groups. Instruct them to work together to gain a deep understanding of their subtopic. They read, examine, and discuss the material. They can summarize; identify main idea and key points; discuss why people need to know this, how this adds to or relates to what they already know on the topic, and how it is relevant to their lives. They re-read, if needed. They discuss what is important to share with their Home Groups. Each Expert writes down the ideas that will be shared with their Home Group.

Step 2: Teach to Home Groups:

Experts return to Home Groups. Each Home Group will now have someone who is an expert on each one of the subtopics of the assignment. It will be each Expert's job to teach the important ideas of his or her subtopic. All students take notes and summarize what they learn from each Expert. Members of the Home Group can ask the Experts questions to clarify ideas.

Step 3: Back to Expert Groups for Deeper understanding:

At this point, the teacher can give all students or all groups the complete article, poem, diagram, video, or other material that comprised the entire topic/assignment. Back in Expert Groups, students discuss how their part fits the whole larger topic. What does their part contribute? Why is it necessary? How does it relate to each of the other parts? How do all the parts work together for important understandings? **This is the step where students use metacognitive skills to arrive at their deepest understanding of the entire topic**.

> ***Alternate approach:*** At the end of this step, groups might use (or create) large jigsaw puzzle pieces to display some key ideas they've gleaned about how the parts relate to the whole. The teacher can provide large puzzle pieces. OR, each group could begin with a large piece of mural paper and treat it as a whole puzzle. Cut it into the number of jigsaw pieces as you have Expert Groups. Each Expert Group writes, diagrams, or otherwise depicts a message to explain what their piece lends to the whole topic. Then Expert Groups could put together an actual jigsaw puzzle with these pieces!

Name _____

Putting the Pieces Together

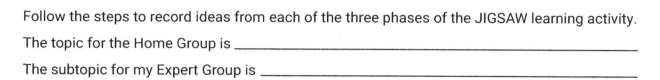

Follow the steps to record ideas from each of the three phases of the JIGSAW learning activity.

The topic for the Home Group is _____

The subtopic for my Expert Group is _____

Step 1: After working with your Expert Group, write 2 or 3 Key ideas/ concepts on which you are now an expert. These are understandings you will share with your Home Group to explain your part of the puzzle.

Step 2: Write key ideas from each of the other Experts who spoke to your Home Group about a subtopic.

Expert Group Subtopic:

Key Idea(s)

Expert Group Subtopic:

Key Idea(s)

Expert Group Subtopic:

Key Idea(s)

Expert Group Subtopic:

Key Idea(s)

Step 3: Back with your Expert Group, discuss and answer these questions.

How does what we learned in our Expert Group fit with the whole topic?

How does it connect or add to each of the other topics to complete the whole message?

Tool 40

REFLECTING ON THE TOOLS

✳ Purpose: Examine personal experience working with the tools in this Achievement Pillar

👤 User(s): Leaders, teachers

📚 Leader Resource:

Building Brilliant Schools by Dr. Andy Parker, (2021), Chapters 11 through 13

📝 Supplies:

Worksheet A.40, Looking Back and Looking Forward
A list of the tools that have been used from this chapter
Results of completed tasks from tools in this chapter

Description:

This tool offers a way for those who have used the tools in this section to reflect on what they have done and learned. In addition, it inspires a look forward as to what concepts, behaviors, or goals they will develop and use in the future.

Steps:

1. Distribute copies of **Worksheet A.40, Looking Back and Looking Forward**, as a guide. Also provide a list of the tools that have been used by individuals or groups in their work together. In addition, if the folks reflecting have saved any products or worksheets from the individual tools—these would be helpful to have on hand as participants reflect over their experiences.

2. With the worksheet as a guide, individuals reflect on their own and note their reflections. If students have used some of the tools, you might invite them to do the same or similar process of reflection.

3. Depending on the setting, groups may choose to share and discuss their reflections. Teams or grade-level groups or entire faculties may wish to use the reflections to set goals together.

Name _____

Looking Back and Looking Forward

Reflect on what you learned, thought, experienced, and wish to do further with the tools in this pillar. Write a comment in each category.

Most powerful tool for me, and why	
Most challenging tool for me, and why	
A key idea I learned	
Tool that I think will be great for my students, and why	
Tool that's been most helpful to my group of colleagues, and why	
Something I learned about myself while using these tools	
Two goals I want to set for myself related to the tools in this pillar	

Chapter 5

Tools for Your TENACITY Toolbox

It's not that I'm so smart. It's just that I stay with problems longer.
– Albert Einstein, German Physicist

This collection of tools focuses on the traits, skills, or practices that have been identified, through good research, as key influences on the development of academic tenacity.

⚙ Definitions

Academic Tenacity: *the **mindsets** and **skills** that allow students to*

(1) *look beyond short-term concerns to **longer-term or higher-order goals**, and*

(2) ***withstand challenges and setbacks** to persevere toward these goals.*
*The **non-cognitive factors** that promote long-term learning and achievement can be brought together under the label 'academic tenacity.' At its most basic level, academic tenacity is about **working hard**, and **working smart**, for a **long time**.* (Dweck et al., 2014, p. 4)

Notice the bolded words and phrases to catch a glimpse of the depth of this concept! Academic tenacity is not about intelligence. It is a personal quality (or a set of combined qualities) that is positively associated with high achievement.

⚙ Key Benefits of Academic Tenacity

Tenacious learners (in comparison to those who are less so) are more likely to

• Achieve academically to their best potential

• Believe in themselves to take on the tasks (higher academic self-efficacy)

• Demonstrate a growth mindset

• See difficulties and setbacks as opportunities to learn rather than as signs of failure or their lack of ability

• Set long-term goals and be willing to work hard to pursue them

• Avoid looking for the easy way out; stay open to academic challenges

• Use long-term self-regulation strategies to keep motivated and stay committed

• Use self-control to avoid distractions (external and internal)

• Have coping skills to handle normal stressors

- Believe in the value of their contributions; believe that effort is worthwhile—that their persistence will get them to their goals

- See school as relevant to their future

- Have a sense of connectedness (belonging) at school

- Be unafraid of self-reflection and self-evaluation

- Seek input and feedback from others

- Be open to considering new ideas and taking academic risks

- Look beyond the immediate rewards to longer-term rewards

- Have an orientation toward learning rather than toward performance

- Know when to quit and modify a quest or to change strategies

The above list gives us an idea of the positive outcomes—gifts we can offer students when we teach and live with them in a school culture that conscientiously nurtures tenacity. As each of the identified attitudes, skills, and characteristics grows, it—in turn—strengthens tenacity. It's a cause-effect-cause relationship.

⚙ Influences on Academic Tenacity

We'd like for all of our students to be academically tenacious—right? Yet speeches about working harder, staying on task, sticking with a project, not giving up (*i.e.,* being tenacious) don't necessarily work to develop tenacity in students! **The good news is that tenacity can be learned**. Yes, perhaps some of your students walk into your classrooms already armed with a good measure of tenacity. But for the others—all is not lost. Here are some of the factors (and skills we can teach) found to have positive influence on the development of academic tenacity:

- Growth mindset

- Self-efficacy

- Self-regulation

- Belonging

- Quality relationships

- Social skills

- Learning to set and pursue long-term and higher-order goals

- A rigorous and supportive learning environment

- Intentional teaching of strategies that support tenacity

- Continual practice of gratitude

⚙ Obstacles to Tenacity

Research (as well as the experience of many teachers) teaches us that such factors and situations as these get in the way of building academic tenacity:

- Lack of adequate amounts of the above positive influences

- Adult efforts to remove or minimize difficulties for students

- Media messages that give false ideas about what it takes to achieve

- The "instant" gratification of finding things on the Internet—without having to research, analyze, evaluate, or use other thinking skills

- Family trauma

- Social alienation

- Racism and other forms of stereotyping or bias

- Family mobility

- Dangerous neighborhoods

- Poverty

Note: For a more complete discussion of tenacity definitions, benefits, influences, and obstacles, see Chapters 14 through 16 in **Building Brilliant Schools: What G.R.E.A.T. Leaders Do Differently**, by Dr. Andy Parker (2021). Use the next page to keep notes from your reading of those chapters.

⚙ Tenacity Tools for Brilliant Schools

Each of the following tools in this chapter teaches or strengthens one or more of the skills known to nurture academic tenacity.

41. Mindset Seminar (Understand and Examine Mindset)

42. Mindset Comparisons (Compare Fixed and Growth Mindsets)

43. Values Affirmations (Reinforce Integrity and Self-Worth)

44. Praise Revisited (Use of Precise, Process Praise)

45. What's the Question? (Higher-Order Questioning)

46. Belonging Boosters (School Connectedness; Belonging)

47. Tenacity Obstacle Course (Obstacle Management)

48. No-Fear Feedback (Effective Teacher and Peer Feedback)

49. Think It Over! (Student Reflection on Work; Metacognition)

50. Reflecting on the Tools (Self-evaluation of Use of Tenacity Tools)

Notes from Tenacity Chapters

Building Brilliant Schools: What G.R.E.A.T. Leaders Do Differently, Chapters 14–16

As you read about Tenacity, jot down key ideas or points that you want to remember from each chapter.

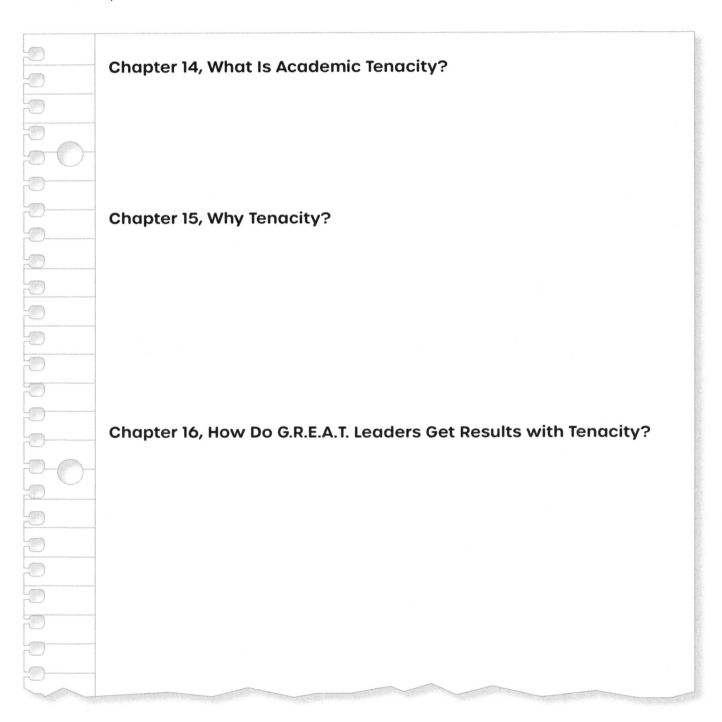

Chapter 14, What Is Academic Tenacity?

Chapter 15, Why Tenacity?

Chapter 16, How Do G.R.E.A.T. Leaders Get Results with Tenacity?

Tool 41

MINDSET SEMINAR

(✳) **Purpose:** Introduce students to the what, why, and how of a growth mindset

(👤) **User(s):** Leaders, teachers, students

(📚) **Leader Resources:**

Building Brilliant Schools by Dr. Andy Parker (2021), Chapters 14 through 16

Background articles, videos, or other resources the teacher has gathered that show mindset information, particularly in student-friendly language and presentation

MindsetWorks website: https://mindsetworks.com/science/

(Short link: https://bit.ly/mindsetworks)

Mindset: The New Psychology of Success, by Carol S. Dweck (2017)

(📝) **Supplies:**

Worksheet T.41, Mindset Notes

Description:

Most educators understand the power of a growth mindset and its connection to achievement. **Without an understanding and incorporation of growth mindset**—the belief that intelligence and other abilities can grow with work and practice—**students cannot develop academic tenacity**.

This tool gives leaders and teachers a strategy to teach students (kids or adult students!) about mindset—what it is and how it makes a difference in the way you see yourself, learn, and approach tasks. Its steps give basic information about mindset and the skills that help to develop a growth mindset.

Steps:

1. As the leader or teacher, consult the above-listed resources and other resources to build your own knowledge about mindset. Gather good articles, posters, or short videos about neuroplasticity and mindset. Find resources that are readily shareable with students.

2. Use resources to plan a seminar (or series of short seminars) to teach the basics of mindset.

3. Distribute copies of **Worksheet T.41, Mindset Notes**, to students. Direct them to use this page for writing key definitions and ideas and for taking other notes or drawing sketches or diagrams as they learn about mindset. Be sure to allow time throughout your presentation(s) for feedback, discussion, questions, and comments.

4. Using good teaching practices and resources (include visuals, stop-and-review practices, stop-and-discuss with partner, real-life examples, connection to what they already know, etc.), include the following topics and activities in your seminar. Give students time to jot notes on the worksheet as you go along.

- Explain that intelligence can be developed—that the brain can rewire itself and develop new skills. Define and discuss *neuroplasticity* and how the brain "gets smarter."

- Describe and discuss the way the brain grows new neural pathways as you use it and as you take on challenges. Students can draw sketches or diagrams on the worksheet to help them remember that the brain can grow new pathways.

- Define, describe, and discuss *fixed mindset*.

- Define, describe, and discuss *growth mindset*.

- Ask students to brainstorm what they think would be benefits of a growth mindset.

- They might also brainstorm some drawbacks of a fixed mindset.

5. Explain that just knowing about a growth mindset or wanting one does not make it happen! Be clear that people can do certain activities and learn skills that help this mindset develop. Explain that these same skills will help them "grow" in academic tenacity. Give a brief overview of some of the skills that you'll work on together:

- Practicing a process or skill—especially with distributed practice. This is repeating something, but with intervals of time between the practices. Taking a break of a few days (or sometimes weeks) helps your brain hold onto the skill longer!

- Practicing metacognition—thinking about and talking about how you think (being aware of, monitoring, and evaluating what you know and don't now and how you learn)

- Making a plan for tackling a problem

- Identifying issues or problems and working together to solve them

- Setting goals and following a plan to reach them

- Identifying obstacles that you might meet in reaching a goal and having ideas ahead of time for getting past the obstacles

- Identifying and correcting mistakes

- Gathering and practicing ways to overcome something you are stuck on

- Planning ways to review and practice something you need to learn or learn how to do

Name _____

Mindset Notes

As you learn about mindset, use these spaces to write key definitions, ideas, questions, and other notes that will help you remember the information.

A fixed mindset is

Neuroplasticity means

A growth mindset is

Benefits of a Growth Mindset

How to Move to a Growth Mindset

Tool 42 MINDSET COMPARISONS

✳ **Purpose:** Explore influences and outcomes of a fixed mindset and a growth mindset

👤 **User(s):** Leaders, teachers, students

📚 **Leader Resource:**

Building Brilliant Schools by Dr. Andy Parker, (2021), Chapters 14 through 16

📝 **Supplies:**

Worksheet T.42, A Look at Two Mindsets
Students' notes from Worksheet T.41 (Mindset Notes, used with Tool 41)
Drawing supplies (pencils, pens, markers, paper)

Description:

A growth mindset is foundational to developing tenacity. Use this tool to dive deeper into understanding the effects of a fixed mindset and a growth mindset. Students discuss questions and complete a comparison chart that encourages thinking about how the two different mindsets lead to ways of thinking about oneself, schoolwork, goals, failure, and other facets of life and school.

Steps:

1. Review with students (including adult students) what they know about the definitions and descriptions of a *fixed mindset* and a *growth mindset*. (They might refer to notes they took on Worksheet T.41 from the previous tool.)

2. Distribute copies of **Worksheet T.42, A Look at Two Mindsets**. Group students in pairs. Review the instructions on the worksheet. Ask them to use their understandings about mindset to complete the chart.

3. Allow time for pairs to discuss and make notes in response to the questions.

4. Join each pair with another pair for students to share and discuss their thoughts.

5. Gather the whole group together to hear key ideas from each foursome.

6. On the same day, or in another session, follow up by having students create scenarios that might happen in school (or that they've seen happen in or out of school)—with peers, or in their own academic work. Role-play how someone might respond to each one from a fixed mindset and from a growth mindset. As an alternative to role-play, students could create a drawing or comic-book-style page to show the scenarios from two different mindset responses.

Name(s) _____

A Look at Two Mindsets

For each question, write words or phrases to describe how a **fixed mindset** would influence that situation or how the person might respond. Then look at the question again, and tell how a **growth mindset** would affect the situation or response.

What does this mindset mean	Fixed Mindset	Growth Mindset
for how you see or think about the work you do?		
for why you do your schoolwork?		
for the level of difficulty or challenge you'd be willing to take on?		
for how much or how well you achieve?		
for what you do when you have difficulty or setbacks?		
for how you view and take criticism?		
for how you view and handle failure?		
for how you compare yourself to how others are doing?		

Tool 43

VALUES AFFIRMATIONS

(✳) **Purpose:** Provide opportunities for students (of all ages) to consider, identify, express, and affirm their most meaningful values

(👤) **User(s):** Leaders, teachers, students

(📚) **Leader Resources:**

Building Brilliant Schools by Dr. Andy Parker, (2021), Chapters 14 through 16
Teacher's list of Sample Values Affirmations (see Worksheet T.43a)

(📝) **Supplies:**

Worksheet T.43a, Sample Values Affirmations
Worksheet T.43b, My Values Affirmations

Description:

Affirmations of one's values has been found to have a strong influence on self-confidence, self-reliance, and academic tenacity. A values-affirmation is any act that reassures people that they have integrity, even in tough situations. Identifying and expressing meaningful values leads to self-evaluation and reflection, combats self-doubts, reduces stress, and supports better performance. This tool offers a strategy for students to reflect on their affirmations (stated values they hold about themselves) and on which are most meaningful and why.

Steps:

1. Give only a brief introduction to students, explaining that they'll be doing a short activity where they will think about what they value in themselves.

2. Distribute copies of **Worksheet T.43b, My Values Affirmations**. Review the components of the page with them.

3. Explain the terms *value* (something about yourself or your life that you find of importance, worth, or benefit—or all three) and *affirmation* (clear confirmation that something is true).

4. If you feel students might need a bit more explanation, you can share some of the ideas from **Worksheet T.43a, Sample Values Affirmations**—not the whole list. Or you can describe the kinds of things that are on it: *personal qualities, abilities, ways you treat people, elements of your self-control or self-care, what you believe about yourself, your strengths, what you deserve, what you're good at, your best characteristics, how hard and well you work, things you're proud of, hard things you're able to do, things you notice that you are improving at doing or being, difficulties you have overcome, etc.*

5. Give students time to work through the questions. If you wish, you might address one element at a time, taking thinking time for each part—1, 2, 3.

Notes to the Teacher or Leader about Tenacity Tool 43:

- This is an easy-to-do strategy. It requires little time.

- This is highly valuable for adults as well as kids! Try it out first (and often) with the staff.

- This can be effective when done without any introductory remarks other than a brief explanation of affirmations and, for some ages, some examples.

- Keep all affirmations private. Don't follow-up with a group discussion unless students would like to talk about the process and what they learned from doing it.

- Never give any grades or correct errors in these.

- It is most powerful as a regular classroom activity. Just explain that it's a good practice to think about ways you value yourself or situations in your life.

- The timing of self-affirmations is important. Research finds that, if a values affirmation is done shortly before a high-anxiety project is due or an important test is taken, it has a strong positive influence on the person's achievement on that activity. This is especially true for students who feel less confident, less included, or less capable.

- As an alternate approach for younger students, give a selection of affirmations already written out and have them choose their top ten or prioritize 1 through 10 in the top ten. This can be followed with a simple note about why number one is the most meaningful or why they identified each one in the top ten.

- This can be used more than once. Repeat it when the timing is right to boost self-confidence before a high-stakes event. Students might want to compare one value affirmations expression with previous ones—to see if priorities have changed. This would be just for their own reflection; but it would also make for interesting sharing and discussion if participants choose to do so.

Sample Values Affirmations

I am capable of doing many things.
I believe in myself.
What I think and say matters.
I choose my own attitude.
I have a positive outlook on life.
I believe I can contribute to the world.
I know that I am worthwhile.
There are ways that I am making a difference.
When I am a leader, I am fair and kind to others.
I feel hopeful for the future.
I have inner strength.
I feel I can be successful.
I am in charge of my own happiness.
I am a good friend.

I am good at including others.
I am a good sport.
I stick up for others.
I can do hard things.
I can survive through disappointments.
I can calm myself.
I know it's okay to make mistakes.
I am able to learn from my mistakes.
I have a good sense of humor.
I don't waste time comparing myself to others.
I have people who love me.
I apologize when I hurt someone.

I have a positive influence on others.
I choose to be around positive people.
I can make healthy choices.
I deserve to be happy.
I feel brave in many situations.
I feel good about how I look.
My opinions and ideas are important.
I am able to treat others respectfully.
I can control how I respond when I'm angry.

I feel I belong at my school (in my class).
I can resolve conflicts with others.
I can keep going when things get hard.
I ask for help when I need it.
I don't give up easily.
I'm a good thinker.
I feel important.
I'm getting better at _____.
I take responsibility for my feelings and actions.
I don't blame others when things don't go well.
I am able to do things independently.
I am an important part of a caring social group.
I approve of myself.
I am creative.
When I hit rough times, I believe they will pass.
I have plenty of brilliant ideas.
I can let go of negative feelings.
I feel confident.
When I fail, I can pick myself up and try again.
I am good at sharing.

I have a great imagination.
I have a lot of energy.
I am able to forgive people.
I can take on a challenge with confidence.
I work hard to take care of myself.
I recognize that I have talents.
I make good use of the talents I have.
I can name many things and people for which/whom I am grateful.
I can let people know I am grateful.
I am grateful for myself.
I don't need to act in mean, rejecting, or superior ways to others.
I draw well (or dance, sing, act, play tennis, skate board, climb, skate, communicate, etc.)

Name _____

My Values Affirmations

Follow the directions to state things about yourself that have worth—qualities, behaviors, attributes, or attitudes that you value about yourself and your life.

1. What do you value about yourself?
List some that are meaningful to you.

_____   _____
_____   _____
_____   _____
_____   _____
_____   _____
_____   _____
_____   _____

2. Which are most important of all the values?
Identify the top three that are most important. Label them 1, 2, 3.

3. Why is it meaningful?
Choose one or two from your top three.

WHY I Chose Number _____   WHY I Chose Number _____

Tool 44
PRAISE REVISITED

✳ **Purpose:** Rethink the kind of praise given to students; expand use of process praise

👤 **User(s):** Leaders, teachers

📚 **Leader Resources:**

Building Brilliant Schools by Dr. Andy Parker, (2021), Chapters 14 through 16

Tips for Praise (see next page)

Teacher-gathered articles and resources about the use of praise

Article by Carol S. Dweck (2007), "The Perils and Promises of Praise"

https://www.ascd.org/el/articled/the-perils-and-promises-of-praise

(Short link: https://bit.ly/csdweck)

📝 **Supplies:**

Worksheet T.44, Our Process-Praise Bank

Description:

Some praise helps kids learn. Other kinds do not. We teachers frequently use praise to encourage and reward academic work. Many researchers today are teaching us that the most common forms of praise *(Good job! You're so good at this! How smart you are!)* are not the right way to do it. Carol Dweck (2007), who researches mindset, motivation, and tenacity, argues that praise which gives the message that intelligence is the major cause of achievement is **downright harmful**. Such praise comes out of a fixed mindset—the idea that cognitive ability is inherent and fixed. This squashes motivation even for the highest achievers.

Instead of praising an outcome or for being smart, praise for effort and for using academic skills. This leaves students confident and eager, says Dweck. Research shows that students praised for effort (rather than outcomes) show strong performances and greater improvement. Dweck calls this *process praise*—it's praise for engagement, perseverance, strategies, improvement, and the like. It tells students precisely what they've done to be successful and what they need to do to be successful again in the future. **Process praise underpins and bolsters tenacity.** It fosters motivation, increased effort, willingness to take on new challenges, greater self-confidence, and a higher level of success.

Using this tool, educators will examine their "praise habits," and build a collection of praise expressions that boost tenacity and higher achievement.

Steps:

1. Strengthen your background on the topic of praise. Do some research, gather articles, and collaborate with colleagues to examine the latest research and good advice on praise. Read the Dweck article cited on the previous page. Share and discuss this with colleagues.

2. Do a quick self-assessment of the kind of praise you use most often. Jot down a few of your most frequently-used statements. For one week, keep track of how often you praise and how you do it. (Ask your students to keep tallies of the number of times you say "Good job!")

3. Join with your team-members or a few colleagues to complete **Worksheet T.44, Our Process-Praise Bank**. Some effort praise or process praise may be specific to your subject area. So, it may work well for you to join with teachers who teach the same content. That is—gather praise ideas for math work, writing, reading tasks, physical education activities, musical practice, etc.

4. Add to the collection regularly. Take note of good uses of praise that you hear from other teachers, leaders, parents, or friends. Ask students to let you know what feedback from you helps them grow and learn better.

Make sure that your praise . . .

IS SPECIFIC, PRECISE—*Example: You put your knowledge of how to solve one-step equations to good use, expanding it to tackle two-step equations.*

IS HELPFUL—*Example: Your use of mental math tricks worked great on that first set of problems. Let's talk about another strategy that might have worked better for you on that second group. Those were a bit stickier.*

ENCOURAGES TRYING NEW THINGS—*Example: You had a rough start on this project, but you changed tactics, refined the goals a bit, and stuck with it. I noticed how you got around some roadblocks by telling yourself, "I can do this!" **Example:** That came easily for you. I think you're ready for the challenge of some more sophisticated vocabulary tasks. Let's try this . . .*

IS FOCUSED ON THE PROCESS—*Example: Highlighting the question in the problem helps to remember what it is you're being asked to find. Highlighting the three facts that you had to work with was another great move. These are good strategies for clarifying the problem.*

IS SINCERE—Kids know when praise is phony or is an automatic habit. If they don't believe you, they'll feel even worse about their work. Don't let your praise become empty. The more thought you give to specific praise, the more it is likely to be sincere.

Name(s) _____

Our Process-Praise Bank

Collect phrases, words, statements, sentence-starters, and actions that praise effort, process, and tactics rather than outcomes or inherent talents.

Good Examples of Effort/Process Praise

YES!

Avoid This Praise!

NO!

Tool 45

WHAT'S THE QUESTION?

(✳) **Purpose:** Help students learn to ask questions that will enable them to learn better

 User(s): Leaders, teachers, students

 Leader Resource:

Building Brilliant Schools by Dr. Andy Parker (2021), Chapters 14 through 16

📝 **Supplies:**

Worksheet T.45a, Questioner's Guide
Worksheet T.45b, Questions to Stretch the Brain
Pad of (good-sized) sticky notes for each pair of students

Description:

Good questioning is one of the specific strategies that develops tenacity. Asking questions and figuring out answers to questions is at the heart of learning in all content areas. Students encounter hundreds of questions a day! However,

- many (perhaps too many) of those questions are "closed-ended" (there is a single answer or a set group of answers; the question promotes limited response) rather than "open-ended" (questions that encourage individuals to higher-level thinking, wondering, coming to conclusions, expressing their own viewpoints and seeking others' viewpoints).

- most of the questions are asked by the teachers. (Some research has found that, in most classrooms, teachers ask 95% of the questions.)

Open-ended questions spark minds and challenge students. As they work out answers, they become aware of their own thinking, and you learn about how they think. But students need to be taught to ask questions as well. In order to generate a question, the student must think about the concept, make sense of it, connect it to what they know, and clearly identify what it is they want to learn. Questioning also builds social connections with peers and adults as students receive and process the responses to their questions.

This tool introduces students to some skills and examples to learn to ask the right kinds of questions that will stretch their brains and expand knowledge. The strategy is focused on students, but leaders and teachers can use it to expand their use of thought-provoking questions. Use it again and again as a kickoff or culmination for a variety of lessons. This might be a two-session tool: use steps 1–5 in one session and 6–7 in one or more other sessions.

Steps:

1. Give a mini-lesson on kinds of questions. Introduce students to the idea of *closed-ended* and *open-ended* questions. Show or read some examples; ask students to distinguish between the different types. *How many answers do you think this question has? What kind of thinking process will you need to do to answer this question? Does this question challenge you to dig deeper into the topic? Would everyone answer this question the same way?*

2. Let students know that asking and answering open-ended questions helps to stretch their thinking. It pushes them to examine and analyze information and to understand the ideas better. When they listen to answers of others, they benefit from different opinions and new insights. Tell them that they'll be building the skills of asking and answering questions that invite exploration, creative thinking, and expression of individual viewpoints or ideas.

3. Have students work in pairs for 5 minutes (set a timer) to brainstorm a few examples of closed-ended questions. Then give them another few minutes to select 1 to 3 closed-ended questions, write each on a sticky note, and stick them up on the walls.

4. Use the information on **Worksheet T.45a, Questioner's Guide**, as appropriate for the grade level. You might share some or all of the tips and sample questions.

5. Set the timer again for 5 minutes. Each student selects a sticky note from a wall, takes it down, and writes an open-ended question to replace it. (For example: *What is the answer to the first problem? . . .*could become *How did you arrive at the answer to that problem* OR, *How do you know your answer is correct?*) Take time to share some of these in the group.

6. Use the graphic organizer, **Worksheet T.45b, Questions to Stretch the Brain**, and work individually or in pairs. The center box is the place to write an idea, opinion, topic, statement, or concept (or to write a brief description of the assignment or text) that will be the focal point for generating questions. Use the remaining spaces and lines to write open-ended questions that will help get to the deeper understandings or insights about the topic.

7. Take time for pairs to share some of their questions. Then spend some time answering them!

Questioner's Guide

Tips for Questioning

Ask questions that

- challenge others to begin thinking about something
- ask people to connect ideas (relate one thing to another)
- trigger individuals to express their own interpretations
- show your curiosity (or trigger someone else's) about a topic
- nudge someone to reflect on someone else's idea or opinion
- invite others to give examples of a concept
- inspire kids to get into discussions with each other
- ask you to identify the most important part of a concept
- ignite ideas you really want to listen to and think about
- probe deeper into the Why? and How? of a topic
- show your interest in hearing other people's viewpoints
- spark someone to figure out how something works
- prompt others to ask open-ended questions
- help you expand your understanding of something you already know a little about

Some Questions to Ask

Why?

Why not?

What's the point?

How can this be verified?

How does this work?

Why does this matter?

How do you know this?

What are the benefits?

What are the consequences?

Where else can I apply this?

What is confusing to me?

How are the consequences greater than the benefits?

Where else have I seen something like this?

What difference does this make in the world (or for me)?

What assumptions are behind that claim (position)?

What's missing in this argument (or description)?

Is the information reliable? How can you tell?

Which of the messages is most important (and why)?

How does this compare to _____?

What does the speaker want me to believe?

If _____ is true, then what about _____?

If _____ is not true, then what does that mean for_____?

How does this change _____?

What would I need to verify this?

How can we break this down into steps?

What are some other options?

In what other situations is this useful?

What other way could this be solved?

How is this author thinking about ____?

How could you apply ____ to _____?

What is the evidence for this?

How can I explain this to someone else?

How did you go about solving this?

How might someone else view this?

Why did you decide to use this strategy?

Name _____

Questions to Stretch the Brain

In the center starburst shape, write the idea, assignment, opinion, topic, or text that will be the focus of the questions. Around the page, write questions that will help get to deeper meanings of the topic. Focus on *Why? Why not? How? What if?* and *Where else?* questions.

Tool 46

Belonging Boosters

⊛ **Purpose:** Increase awareness of belonging and strengthen belongingness

👤 **User(s):** Leaders, teachers, students

📚 **Leader Resource:**

Building Brilliant Schools by Dr. Andy Parker (2021), Chapters 14 through 16

📝 **Supplies:**

Worksheet T.46a, Ways to Bolster Belonging
Worksheet T.46b, Belonging Diary

Description:

Belonging is the perception a person has of being accepted, included, and valued in a particular setting. It's one of those basic human needs. Every school day, beginning (on the bus or on the school grounds) even before the first bell rings and lasting throughout the day, students carry a sense of whether or not they belong to their school and their classes. **Belonging at school looms large as a contributor to developing academic tenacity.** At the same time, experiences and feelings of not belonging are huge impediments to academic tenacity. Belonging has major ramifications in a school setting for students' academic performance, self-esteem, social connections, and overall wellbeing.

This tool reviews some of the proven practices and conditions that increase belonging. In addition, the strategy of keeping a "belonging diary" gives students opportunities to increase awareness of belonging (how it looks and feels), become aware of **lack** of belonging (how it looks and feels), and find (and practice) ways to boost belonging for themselves and others.

Steps:

1. For leaders and teachers: Review the list of verified belonging boosters on **Worksheet T.46a, Ways to Bolster Belonging.** Then use that page as a way and place to consider your own behaviors and practices related to the belonging-ness of students and others in the school. Let this worksheet inspire you to take specific steps to attend to belonging and to intentionally work toward making your classroom and school a place where all students and adults can feel they belong.

2. For teachers working with students: When you feel you have gained understanding of what belonging is, why it is important, and how to help it flourish—begin discussing the topic with your students. Let them talk (in pairs, small groups, or the whole group) about what it means, why it's important, what are the benefits (and drawbacks of NOT feeling you belong), what helps someone belong, how belonging can be increased in school, etc.

3. Tell students that one way to improve belonging for everyone is to increase awareness of it (and the lack of it), of what it means, and of how it happens. Using **Worksheet T.46b, Belonging Diary**, is a way for them to become "belonging investigators." Challenge students to keep their senses tuned to belonging. Then once or twice a week, they'll make an entry in a Belonging Diary. (Use the worksheet; or students can create digital diaries or any other form.) This might be a 5-minute task at a time you determine. Entries are for jotting down anything they have noticed or thought about on the topic of belonging. Share these suggestions below and encourage students to contribute others. Re-show this each time they are ready to write.

   • Answer such a question as one of these with your thoughts for that day:
   What does belonging mean to you? Why does it matter? How does it feel to belong (or not to belong)?

   • Or notice and write about

   A time or situation in which you feel you belong (or feel you don't)
   A time or situation in which you can tell someone else has a sense of belonging
   Something that you see has harmed a person's sense of belonging
   A teacher or other adult doing something that helps someone belong
   Examples of belonging among the adults in the school
   Something that helps your family feel a sense of belonging at school
   How or when belonging or not belonging affects your schoolwork (or someone else's)
   Obstacles that you notice interfere with belonging
   What a sense of belonging helps or enables you to do
   Something you do to increase your sense of belonging
   Something you did to boost someone else's sense of belonging
   Your ideas for things that the teacher can do to boost belonging in the classroom
   Your ideas for things classmates can do to boost belonging in the class
   Your ideas for school-wide practices that can boost belonging

4. Now and then, students can select a thought, idea, or question from their diaries—to contribute to a class discussion. (Make this optional.)

Name _____

Ways to Bolster Belonging

These practices increase awareness and experiences of belonging in your school and classroom. Use this checklist to monitor your work on better belonging. Note dates when you do intentional act or process to strengthen this. Put a check in the first column when this has become a consistent, continuing practice.

✓	Practice or Condition	Dates
	Caring, trusting student-teacher relationships	
	Attention to building positive peer-to-peer relationships	
	Effective, proactive classroom management	
	Clear and consistently-enforced expectations for respectful behavior	
	No-nonsense, consistently-followed, zero-tolerance policies for harassment, discrimination, or demeaning of any sort	
	Teachers showing that they welcome, value, and embrace all students, and that they will offer equal access to resources and help	
	Evidence that all students (and staff) have equal opportunities to share perspectives, opinions, and ideas	
	A learning environment that is safe, emotionally and physically	
	Teaching of learning strategies that boost students' tenacity, academic self-view, and chances for academic success (such as goal setting, goal accomplishment, problem-solving, reflection on work processes, dealing with obstacles and failure, giving and receiving feedback; and skills of questioning, listening, organizing, summarizing, reviewing)	
	Regular, intentional teaching of skills that increase belonging (cooperative learning skills, listening skills, communication skills, social skills, self-management skills)	
	Frequent opportunities for students to work in cooperative groups	
	DYNAMIC learning activities—engaging and relevant to students	
	Assuring that each student experiences some academic success **daily**	
	Repeated experiences of competence and autonomy for students	
	Conversations with colleagues about belonging	
	Frequent conversations with students about belonging	
	Intentional practices to help students' families experience belonging	
	Targeted teaching of academic skills needed to successfully navigate school	
	Evidence of belief that all students are capable of reaching high expectations	
	Regular, ongoing gratitude practices in the school and classrooms	

Belonging Diary

Add entries to record your experiences, thoughts, analyses, questions, ideas, observations, or suggestions about belonging for yourself or others in the school.

Dear Diary,   Date_____

Dear Diary,   Date_____

Dear Diary,   Date_____

Dear Diary,   Date_____

How can I help others feel they belong?

An example of belonging that I observed . . .

How does belonging increase?

Someone did this to help me belong . . .

Something I could do to increase my own sense of belonging . . .

What is belonging?

What does a sense of belonging enable me to do?

How does it feel?

Why does it matter?

Tool 47   TENACITY OBSTACLE COURSE

⊛ **Purpose:** Identify obstacles to tenacity; plan to get around obstacles

 User(s): Leaders, teachers, students

 Leader Resource:

Building Brilliant Schools by Dr. Andy Parker (2021), Chapters 14 through 16

📝 **Supplies:**

Worksheet T.47, Obstacle-Course Plan

Multiple pieces of 8.5 x 11-inch posterboard (approximate size)

Markers, masking tape, colored tape, scissors

A large space—such as classroom, gym, cafeteria corner, part of a hallway

Assorted obstacles (chairs, stack of books, shoes, movable desks, backpacks, low step, rope, hoop to crawl through, etc.)

Description:

A key facet of tenacity is dealing with obstacles to progress. These can be interruptions, disruptions, setbacks, loss of interest, emotional barriers, lack of the right materials or resources, relationship issues, fear, or other types of obstacles. Students (and adults) will meet obstacles. So, they need to learn to face them head on. Part of handling obstacles is

- Anticipating them (not being caught by surprise)

- Knowing that it is not the end of the world

- Having (and practicing) some tools or strategies in your pocket for dealing with them

- Having a general (or specific) plan for how to get around them

This active strategy uses an actual physical obstacle-course to help students learn a process for overcoming obstacles. Along with the activity, a template gives a planning form that students can use to anticipate and plan for obstacles that may arise when they work toward a goal. This tool works best with a medium-term goal (something that takes a fair amount of time—such as an assignment that takes a few work sessions). However, younger students might find something like this helpful for an assignment that would be done during one class period.

Steps:

1. With students, discuss and define the word "obstacle." Let students brainstorm about what comes to their minds when they hear the word. Give them a chance to demonstrate or draw ideas as they explain what the word means to them.

2. Ask students to think about obstacles to the academic tenacity it takes to get a school task done or to accomplish an academic goal. **This means roadblocks or impediments (things that get in the way) to their continuing efforts to work hard and work smart for as long as it takes to finish the task well.** Ask them to think about situations, materials needed, problems, factors, feelings, external influences, or internal influences (e.g., past experiences, beliefs, biases, or attitudes) that might be obstacles. Brainstorm ideas together. After general brainstorming, students will be ready to make a plan to handle obstacles in the context of a specific task, assignment, or project.

3. Choose a task that all students will be doing. This can be any kind of work, for example: a visual book report, demonstration of how to solve a particular problem, dramatic performance, informative poster, science experiment, speech, etc.

4. Distribute copies of **Worksheet T.47, Obstacle-Course Plan**, to students. Discuss the two categories shown on the sheet—external and internal obstacles. Students work in groups of 2 or 3 to identify obstacles that could arise. They write these in the left-hand column(s) under "Name the obstacle." Remind the students to think about various kinds of obstacles.

5. After about 10 minutes, share results with the class. There are likely to be duplicate ideas. Select about 10 to 15 obstacles. Supply each group with 2 poster boards. Assign each group one or two obstacles. They write each on a poster in large, readable letters.

6. Now it's time to set up the obstacle course. (You could set this up ahead of time or kids can create it.) Use obstacles to make a "course" around the room. Be sure that students can either walk around or hop over (or climb under) each one. Number the posters. Tape one to each obstacle (in numerical order). Mark a path with colored tape or arrows taped to the floor.

7. The next step is to plan how they will get past the obstacles. Explain the importance of having strategies "in your pocket" before you run into a roadblock. Ask students to think of techniques they've used before, and responses to "glitches" that they have seen others take –as well as new, creative ideas. They write these on **Worksheet T.47, Obstacle-Course Plan**.

8. It's time to "run" the course. There are many ways to do this. Here's one: If there are 15 obstacles, assign a number 1–15 to each student (including yourself). Each takes a turn doing the obstacle course. One at a time—students go through the course (maneuvering all the obstacles that do not have their number). But the student must STOP (get hung up!) at the obstacle with the number assigned. The student stops, reads the obstacle aloud, and gives an idea for how to get around it. If needed, any student may call on someone to help with the thinking or invite alternate ideas. (Student can then finish the course with no more stops.) Continue with another group until all students have run the course.

9. When all have had a turn, many ideas will have been suggested. Students return to small groups. They collaborate to complete the right-hand columns on the worksheet.

10. Later, students can use the worksheet again to reflect back on the obstacles that they did encounter when doing that task. Take some time for the class to give feedback on the entire activity—what they learned, how helpful it was to plan for obstacles, etc. Were they able to use some of their plans for meeting obstacles? This worksheet can become a tool that is used many times in approaching all kinds of assignments and projects.

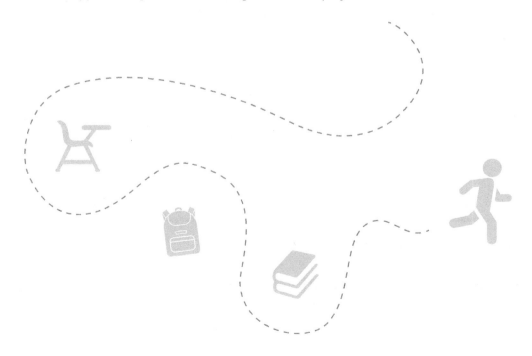

Name _____ Date _____

Obstacle-Course Plan

Assignment or Task: _____

Name some obstacles that might get in the way of keeping going or doing your best.

▶ ## External Obstacles

Name the obstacle	Strategies to use for getting past it

▶ ## Internal Obstacles

Name the obstacle	Strategies to use for getting past it

When you're done with the assignment:

Put an **X** by obstacles that did arise.

Put a **Y** beside the strategy that worked or **N** beside any one that did not.

What conclusions would you draw about what worked?

What would you differently in your planning next time?

Tool 48

NO-FEAR FEEDBACK

Purpose: Learn criteria, processes, and skills for effective feedback

User(s): Leaders, teachers, students

Leader Resource:

Building Brilliant Schools by Dr. Andy Parker (2021), Chapters 14 through 16

Supplies:

Worksheet T.48a, Feedback Must-Haves—A Checklist
Worksheet T.48b, Peer Quick-Note Feedback

Description:

We remove a spark that could light up tenacity if we fail to make regular, useful feedback a part of every student's school experience. The processes of giving and getting feedback help anyone look closely at how they work and think. This is essential to making improvements in learning strategies. Students need feedback on academic tasks from teachers and from peers. They need to be taught how to give it and receive it.

This tool is designed to guide teachers' thinking about feedback, to help teachers plan strategies for teaching feedback skills to students, and to promote steps for students to practice giving helpful feedback to one another. All the steps are applicable to leaders and teachers in their feedback to each other and anyone in the school community.

Steps:

1. Review the ideas and advice on the Worksheet **T.48a, Feedback Must-Haves: A Checklist.**
   Then start (or continue) the process of teaching good feedback by modeling it. Make sure your feedback meets the "musts" on this list! As you give verbal or written feedback to students, explain what you are doing and why—thereby introducing them to the language of feedback (the bold words on the checklist).

2. When students have seen several modeled examples of effective feedback from you, start a conversation with them about how to give feedback. Address the idea that feedback might feel a bit awkward at first; but assure them that the point of feedback is to help them feel proud of what they have done well and give them ideas about what they can do better.

3. Use the checklist on **Worksheet T.48a, Feedback Must-Haves—A Checklist**, as your guide for what to cover with students. Explain the elements of good feedback in language appropriate to the grade level. Give examples of responses that meet each of the must-haves. For example, compare vague statements with specific, helpful feedback.

    Vague: *Great job!*
    Helpful: *From your explanation it was clear to see exactly how you solved the problem.*

    Vague: *This needs more work.*
    Helpful: *The section in the middle of the song felt rushed; the words were hard to catch. Could you sing it again, slowing down a bit and enunciating the words more clearly?*

    Vague: *I liked the ending!*
    Helpful: *The words you chose for the last two lines helped you end your poem with humor. This made me laugh!*

4. Form pairs or small groups. Supply an anonymous short work (a math problem solved and explained, a paragraph written, a video clip of a student explaining steps in an experiment, etc.—things created by you or samples from previous classes). Explain the assignment and the requirements or criteria given before the piece was created. Ask students to work together to write three helpful feedback statements. Use this kind of practice several times.

5. Gradually work up to having students work in pairs to give verbal feedback or written feedback to each other. See **Worksheet T.48b, Peer Quick-Notes Feedback**, for a way that peers can give prompt, brief but effective feedback. After each experience, allow time for students to give feedback on the feedback. The receivers can tell what helped, how they felt receiving the feedback, what they did with suggestions, and what they think would improve the process. Students should do the same with teacher feedback—tell you what was helpful, missing, not helpful, confusing, intimidating, etc.

6. Even the best feedback won't help much if students don't have a time to go back and make improvements to the work using what they learned from the feedback. This is a wonderful process of critical thinking, self-evaluation, self-improvement, and **yes—tenacity**! Listening to others' ideas and deciding what is valuable and using it to make your work better—this is a great "working smart" strategy. And it's an example of "keeping at it"—not settling for a "just-okay" outcome, but pushing on to put in more work and making it better!

Name _____

Feedback Must-Haves— A Checklist

✓	Feedback should be	
	Purposeful	Know the purpose of feedback: to help people improve their work and their work processes. You look for what is done well and make suggestions about what they might be do to improve.
	Fair	It's only fair to respond to or evaluate work according to the requirements for the work. Don't criticize someone for not doing something if that wasn't part of the assignment! Make sure you know the criteria before you begin the work or begin giving feedback on the work. Then give feedback equitably. It's not fair to be hard on some students and give others an easy response.
	Kind	Never be harsh, mean, or demeaning. Never make fun of someone's work or mistakes. Ask questions and give observations with kindness and care. Make statements that build and encourage learners.
	Honest	Don't say something just to say something. Don't just give general praise. Tell what you see. Do it kindly. Your goal is to affirm the other person and help them see the possibilities for what else they can do.
	Specific	Describe the parts, steps, or words that worked well: *The opening paragraph of your story was so suspenseful that I held my breath.* Identify a clear sentence, part of the problem, or place in the diagram that is confusing: *If you go back to this spot and add a step of combining the like terms in the equation, I think you'll find the right solution. It seems that you skipped that step.*
	Actionable	Make comments that a student can actually put to work—noting what worked well so as to keep doing it, and giving concrete ideas of what to do **next** to make the work better.
	Positive	Make positive statements. This shows your growth mindset and your belief in the person's ability to make this work the best possible. Even with suggestions for improvement, the students should hear that you believe they can make good changes.
	Timely	Give feedback as soon as possible after the task is done. Fresh feedback is the kind that works best.
	Cooperative	Encourage dialogue. The feedback giver and feedback receiver can question and respond to each other. This is the best way to get to some good tactics for making the product better.
	Nonjudgmental	Judgments give moral opinions about the value of something. They are subjective—not based on evidence. Good feedback looks at how you did something in light of standards or criteria for doing it well. They point to specific examples of things done well or needing improvements.

Peer Quick-Notes Feedback

After watching, hearing, or reading any academic "performance" or "product" by a peer—whether it is in progress or in its final form—a student gives quick but meaningful notes of feedback.

To the teacher:

• To use the form below, make copies for students. (You or students can design your own.)

• Or students can write on index cards, large sticky notes, or even create digital messages. If you're not using a prepared form, give clear criteria about what the quick-notes should include.

• Tell students to be mindful of what they have learned about the "Musts" of feedback as they write their notes. (See **Worksheet T.48a, Feedback Must-Haves—A Checklist**).

• Adapt the criteria to fit the assignment.

• Have peers write these notes **right away** after a student shares a performance or product.

Peer Quick-Notes Feedback

To _____ From _____

Here's what I thought you did best:

Here's why I think this:

Here's something I noticed that you might work on:

Maybe think about doing this:

Tool 49

THINK IT OVER!

✳ **Purpose:** Give students strategies for and practice in reflecting on their own work

👤 **User(s):** Leaders, teachers, students

📚 **Leader Resource:**

Building Brilliant Schools by Dr. Andy Parker (2021), Chapters 14 through 16

📝 **Supplies:**

Worksheet T.49a, Questions that Spark Reflection
Worksheet T.49b, Reflecting on My Work

Description:

Metacognition is a critical learning skill associated with academic tenacity. It is *becoming aware of your own thought processes and having the ability to analyze how you think*. And self-reflection activities are powerful metacognitive strategies.

Reflect means to *think again*, or *think back on*. In truth, students often have after-thoughts when they finish something: They think they did a great job. They think they failed. They are glad the test (or assignment, or class) is over. In their minds, they recount what they missed. They think the task (or assignment, or class) was a waste of time, or they never want to think about that assignment again!

But we want to invite them to another kind of after-thought: the kind of reflection and collaboration that helps them learn and improve. We also want the kind of reflection that leads to satisfaction and boosts their feelings about themselves as students—and ultimately feeds tenacity. They see the growth, so they're inspired to press on! This tool supplies questions that can be used to help learners build the habit of noticing, communicating, and analyzing ways they think and the processes they use as they learn or accomplish a task. A self-reflection template can be used to evaluate work during the task or after completion.

Steps:

1. Teach students about *metacognition*. Define it. Define *reflection*. Let them make the connection between the two meanings. Kids love to learn about metacognition. First of all, it's a great word to fling around. They're fascinated to realize that they can think about (analyze, evaluate, explore) their own thinking.

2. Secondly, it's even more fascinating for kids to **do** it—to put metacognition into practice. There are dozens of questions that you can ask to trigger learners to think about their own thinking or about the way they did (or are doing) their work. Once they get the idea of how this works, you can help them build the habit of asking the questions of themselves. They can also help each other reflect on their work. These apply well to group work, as well.

3. See **Worksheet T.49a, Questions that Spark Reflection**, for some suggestions of questions that promote reflection. Invite students to add more to the list. You do the same. Some questions will be specific to content areas. Think about what questions instigate reflection in your particular subject and class. Note also that reflection is not solely for completed tasks. It's helpful to do periodic, short reflections on how things are going mid-task. This gives students a chance to consider alternate strategies and time management. It gives the teacher a chance to make suggestions, help find ways to get around obstacles, correct patterns or mistakes that will grow larger as they continue working, or steer students in a more productive direction.

4. Create a template or form to guide students' self-reflections. Use fewer questions for younger students. After doing the process a few times, students can help to design the form. You may find it helpful to have a few different forms—as sometimes the specifics of the reflection are best if attuned to the particular assignment. If you work with younger students, use fewer questions (or statements) or devise a way for them to speak (rather than write) their reflections. **Worksheet T.49b, Reflecting on My Work**, is an example that you can try—or that can inspire you and your students to select questions and create your own.

5. Give students an opportunity to chat with you (the teacher) about some of the points on the reflection page. It's a good chance for you to affirm the metacognitive work, celebrate along with the student for the work and growth, and offer help. Always ask the student, "Is there something you noticed for which I can help? And "How can I help?"

6. Pay attention to obstacles and needs that arise from this information. Notice patterns. Hearing or reading students' reflections may alert you about skills you need to teach or reteach.

Questions that Spark Reflection

Use questions such as these to spark thinking about work habits, progress, patterns, successes, and needs. Add more to the list!

Some questions to ask while you work:

How is it going?

Am I on the right track?

Is there some help I need?

Is this strategy working well?

What other resources would help?

How do I feel about where I am right now?

How am I progressing—given the time constraints?

What else do I need or need to do in order to complete this well?

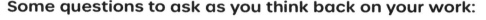

Some questions to ask as you think back on your work:

What skills or strategies did I use here?

What strategies worked well?

What was most successful?

What patterns do I see in my work?

What kinds of mistakes do I see?

How did I deal with obstacles?

How did I manage my time?

What was my best strength here?

What do I need to improve?

What progress have I made?

How can I tell what progress I've made?

What was confusing?

What is still confusing?

How did I feel as I was working on this?

How do I feel now that it is finished?

What process or strategy will I use again?

What is the most effective part of the work I did?

What stretched my brain the most?

How did I manage myself (my attitude, confidence, emotions) during this process?

What setbacks or disruptions did I face?

What am I most proud of about the way I worked?

What mindsets, situations, or other factors affected the way I worked on this?

What did I learn about myself as I did this (about the way I work or think or what my strengths or needs are)?

What skills of mine need more work?

What will I do differently on the next similar assignment?

Name _____ Date _____

Reflecting on My Work

Project or Assignment _____

My best strength for this task was

The most successful strategy I chose was

The most spectacular part of the work or the process was

What challenged me most was

Something I learned about myself while doing this was

After doing this, I feel that I am better at (or understand better)

I'd describe my mindset on this task as

An obstacle that popped up (and how I handled it) was

Something I need to learn, improve, or do differently next time is

On a scale of 1 to 5 (1 being best), I'd give myself a _____ for time management.

On a scale of 1 to 5 (1 being best), I'd give myself a _____ for self-management.

Tool 50
REFLECTING ON THE TOOLS

✳ **Purpose:** Examine personal experience working with the tools in this Tenacity pillar

👤 **User(s):** Leaders, teachers, (students, optional)

📚 **Leader Resource:**

Building Brilliant Schools by Dr. Andy Parker (2021), Chapters 14 through 16

📝 **Supplies:**

Worksheet T.50, Looking Back and Looking Forward
A list of the tools that have been used from this chapter
Results of completed tasks from tools in this chapter

Description:

This tool offers a way for those who have used the tools in this section to reflect on what they have done and learned. In addition, it inspires a look forward as to what concepts, behaviors, or goals they will develop and use in the future.

Steps:

1. Distribute copies of **Worksheet T.50, Looking Back and Looking Forward**, as a guide. Also provide a list of the tools that have been used by individuals or groups in their work together. In addition, if the folks reflecting have saved any products or worksheets from the individual tools—these would be helpful to have on hand as they reflect over their experiences.

2. With the worksheet as a guide, individuals reflect on their own and note their reflections. If students have used some of the tools, you might invite them to do the same or similar process of reflection.

3. Depending on the setting, groups may choose to share and discuss their reflections. Teams or grade-level groups or entire faculties may wish to use the reflections to set goals together.

Name _____

Looking Back and Looking Forward

Reflect on what you learned, thought, experienced, and wish to do further with the tools in this pillar. Write a comment in each category.

Most powerful tool for me, and why	
Most challenging tool for me, and why	
A key idea I learned	
Tool that I think will be great for my students, and why	
Tool that's been most helpful to my group of colleagues, and why	
Something I learned about myself while using these tools	
Two goals I want to set for myself related to the tools in this pillar	

References

⚙ Chapter 1, Gratitude

Emmons, R. A., & McCullough, M. (2003). Counting blessings versus burdens: An experimental investigation of gratitude and subjective well-being in daily life. *Journal of Personality and Social Psychology, 84,* 377–389.

Froh, J. J., Bono, G., Fan, J., Emmons, R. A., Henderson, K., Harris, C., Leggio, H., & Wood, A. M. (2014). Nice thinking! An educational intervention that teaches children to think gratefully. *School Psychology Review, 43*(2), 132–152.

Howells, K. (2013). *Enhancing teacher relationships and effectiveness through the practice of gratitude.* Teachers Matter. http://www.kerryhowells.com/wp-content/uploads/2013/11/58-Enhancing-teacher-relationships-and-effectiveness-through-the-practice-of-gratitude.pdf

Parker, A. (2021). *Building brilliant schools: What G.R.E.A.T. leaders do differently.* Global Wellness Media.

Siegel, D. J., & Bryson, T. P. (2018). *The yes brain: How to cultivate courage, curiosity, and resilience in your child.* Bantam.

⚙ Chapter 2, Relationships

Lim, H, 2018, *Breaking down barriers between educators and families through technology.* Carnegie Corporation.

Parker, A. (2021). *Building brilliant schools: What G.R.E.A.T. leaders do differently.* Global Wellness Media.

⚙ Chapter 3, Expectations

Bias. *Psychology Today,* (2021). https://www.psychologytoday.com/us/basics/bias

Brophy, J. E., & Good, T. L. (1970). Teachers' communication of differential expectations for children's classroom performance: Some behavioral data. *Journal of Educational Psychology, 61*(5), 365-374.

Devine, P. G., Forscher, P. S., Austin, A. J., & Cox, W. T. (2012). Long-term reduction in implicit race bias: A prejudice habit-breaking intervention. *Journal of Experimental Social Psychology, 48*(6), 1267-1278.

Facing History and Ourselves (2021). *Confirmation and other biases.* https://www.facinghistory.org/resource-library/facing-ferguson-news-literacy-digital-age/confirmation-and-other-biases

Losen, D., Hodson, C., Keith, M. A., Morrison, K, & Belway, S. (2015). *Are we closing the school discipline gap?* UCLA, The Civil Rights Project. https://civilrightsproject.ucla.edu/resources/projects/center-for-civil-rights-remedies/school-to-prison-folder/federal-reports/are-we-closing-the-school-discipline-gap

Losen, D. J., Sun, W., & Keith, M. A. (March, 2017). *Suspended education in Massachusetts: Using days of lost instruction due to suspension to evaluate our schools.* The Civil Rights Project. https://civilrightsproject.ucla.edu/resources/projects/center-for-civil-rights-remedies/school-to-prison-folder/summary-reports/suspended-education-in-massachusetts-using-days-of-lost-instruction-due-to-suspension-to-evaluate-our-schools

Nordell, J. (2021). *The end of bias: How we change our minds.* Granta Publications.

Nordell, J. (May, 2017). Is this how discrimination ends? *The Atlantic.* https://www.theatlantic.com/science/archive/2017/05/unconscious-bias-training/525405/

Nordell, J. (2021). The end of bias: *A beginning: The science and practice of overcoming unconscious bias.* Macmillan.

Parker, A. (2021). *Building brilliant schools: What G.R.E.A.T. leaders do differently.* Global Wellness Media.

Rubie-Davies, C. M., Peterson, E. R., Sibley, C. G., & Rosenthal, R. (2015). A teacher expectation intervention: Modelling the practices of high expectation teachers. *Contemporary Educational Psychology, 40,* 72–85.

Rubie-Davies, C. M., & Rosenthal, R. (2016). Intervening in teachers' expectations: A random effects meta-analytic approach to examining the effectiveness of an intervention. *Learning and Individual Difference, 50,* 83–92.

Starck, J. G., Riddle, T., Sinclair, S., & Warikoo, N. (2020). Teachers are people too: Examining the racial bias of teachers compared to other American adults. *Educational Researcher, 49*(4), 273–284.

⚙ Chapter 4, Achievement

Doran, G., Miller, A., and Cunningham, J. (November, 1981). There's a S.M.A.R.T. way to write management goals and objectives. *Management Review, 70*(11), 35–36.

Hattie, J. (2008). *Visible learning: A synthesis of over 800 meta-analyses relating to achievement.* Routledge.

Hattie, J. (2012). *Visible learning for teachers: Maximize impact on learning.* Routledge.

Hattie, J. (2021). *Visible learning: What works best for learning.* Visible Learning, https://visible-learning.org/

Haughey, D. (2014). *A brief history of SMART goals.* Project SMART. https://www.projectsmart.co.uk/brief-history-of-smart-goals.php

Jigsaw classroom (2022). Social Psychology Network. https://www.jigsaw.org/

Parker, A. (2021). *Building brilliant schools: What G.R.E.A.T. leaders do differently.* Global Wellness Media.

⚙ Chapter 5, Tenacity

Dweck, C. S. (2007). The perils and promises of praise. *Educational Leadership, (65)*2, 34–39.

Dweck, C. S. (2017). *Mindset: The new psychology of success.* Ballantine Books.

Dweck, C. S., Walton, G. M., & Cohen, G. L. (2014). Academic tenacity: *Mindsets and skills that promote long-term learning.* Bill and Melinda Gates Foundation. https://ed.stanford.edu/sites/default/files/manual/dweck-walton-cohen-2014.pdf

Parker, A. (2021). *Building brilliant schools: What G.R.E.A.T. leaders do differently.* Global Wellness Media.

Made in the USA
Coppell, TX
20 March 2023

14490057R00116